Oberlin College
Oberlin, Ohio

Written by Sarah LeBaron von Baeyer

Edited by Meghan Dowdell and Kimberly Moore

Layout by Meryl Sustarsic

D1379356

COLLEGE **PROWLER**®

ISBN # 1-4274-0105-5
ISSN # 1551-0544
© Copyright 2006 College Prowler
All Rights Reserved
Printed in the U.S.A.
www.collegeprowler.com

Last updated 9/12/2007

Special Thanks To: Babs Carryer, Andy Hannah, LaunchCyte, Tim O'Brien, Bob Sehlinger, Thomas Emerson, Andrew Skurman, Barbara Skurman, Bert Mann, Dave Lehman, Daniel Fayock, Chris Babyak, The Donald H. Jones Center for Entrepreneurship, Terry Slease, Jerry McGinnis, Bill Ecenberger, Idie McGinty, Kyle Russell, Jacque Zaremba, Larry Winderbaum, Roland Allen, Jon Reider, Team Evankovich, Lauren Varacalli, Abu Noaman, Mark Exler, Daniel Steinmeyer, Jared Cohon, Gabriela Oates, David Koegler, and Glen Meakem.

Bounce-Back Team: Scott Ewart, Yuuki Shinomiya, and Chris Dawson.

College Prowler®
5001 Baum Blvd.
Suite 750
Pittsburgh, PA 15213

Phone: 1-800-290-2682
Fax: 1-800-772-4972
E-Mail: info@collegeprowler.com
Web Site: www.collegeprowler.com

How this all started...

When I was trying to find the perfect college, I used every resource that was available to me. I went online to visit school websites; I talked with my high school guidance counselor; I read book after book; I hired a private counselor. Sure, this was all very helpful, but nothing really told me what life was like at the schools I cared about. These sources weren't giving me enough information to be totally confident in my decision.

In all my research, there were only two ways to get the information I wanted.

The first was to physically visit the campuses and see if things were really how the brochures described them, but this was quite expensive and not always feasible. The second involved a missing ingredient: the students. Actually talking to a few students at those schools gave me a taste of the information that I needed so badly. The problem was that I wanted more but didn't have access to enough people.

In the end, I weighed my options and decided on a school that felt right and had a great academic reputation, but truth be told, the choice was still very much a crapshoot. I had done as much research as any other student, but was I 100 percent positive that I had picked the school of my dreams?

Absolutely not.

My dream in creating *College Prowler* was to build a resource that people can use with confidence. My own college search experience taught me the importance of gaining true insider insight; that's why the majority of this guide is composed of quotes from actual students. After all, shouldn't you hear about a school from the people who know it best?

I hope you enjoy reading this book as much as I've enjoyed putting it together. Tell me what you think when you get a chance. I'd love to hear your college selection stories.

Luke Skurman
CEO and Co-Founder
lukeskurman@collegeprowler.com

Welcome to College Prowler®

During the writing of College Prowler's guidebooks, we felt it was critical that our content was unbiased and unaffiliated with any college or university. We think it's important that our readers get honest information and a realistic impression of the student opinions on any campus—that's why if any aspect of a particular school is terrible, we (unlike a campus brochure) intend to publish it. While we do keep an eye out for the occasional extremist—the cheerleader or the cynic—we take pride in letting the students tell it like it is. We strive to create a book that's as representative as possible of each particular campus. Our books cover both the good and the bad, and whether the survey responses point to recurring trends or a variation in opinion, these sentiments are directly and proportionally expressed through our guides.

College Prowler guidebooks are in the hands of students throughout the entire process of their creation. Because you can't make student-written guides without the students, we have students at each campus who help write, randomly survey their peers, edit, layout, and perform accuracy checks on every book that we publish. From the very beginning, student writers gather the most up-to-date stats, facts, and inside information on their colleges. They fill each section with student quotes and summarize the findings in editorial reviews. In addition, each school receives a collection of letter grades (A through F) that reflect student opinion and help to represent contentment, prominence, or satisfaction for each of our 20 specific categories. Just as in grade school, the higher the mark the more content, more prominent, or more satisfied the students are with the particular category.

Once a book is written, additional students serve as editors and check for accuracy even more extensively. Our bounce-back team—a group of randomly selected students who have no involvement with the project—are asked to read over the material in order to help ensure that the book accurately expresses every aspect of the university and its students. This same process is applied to the 200-plus schools College Prowler currently covers. Each book is the result of endless student contributions, hundreds of pages of research and writing, and countless hours of hard work. All of this has led to the creation of a student information network that stretches across the nation to every school that we cover. It's no easy accomplishment, but it's the reason that our guides are such a great resource.

When reading our books and looking at our grades, keep in mind that every college is different and that the students who make up each school are not uniform—as a result, it is important to assess schools on a case-by-case basis. Because it's impossible to summarize an entire school with a single number or description, each book provides a dialogue, not a decision, that's made up of 20 different topics and hundreds of student quotes. In the end, we hope that this guide will serve as a valuable tool in your college selection process. Enjoy!

OMID GOHARI ◯ CHRISTINA KOSHZOW ◯ CHRIS MASON ◯ JOEY RAHIMI ◯ LUKE SKURMAN ◯
The College Prowler Team

Table of Contents

Introduction from the Author

Most people, when they think of Northern Ohio, imagine long stretches of corn fields and dreary, cold winters. Although this image is not entirely inaccurate, the rich history and modern-day vitality of Oberlin College makes it an extremely appealing choice for anyone interested in a first-class liberal arts education. Perhaps the most important thing to realize about Oberlin is that rather than providing training in specific careers, the school encourages students to stretch their interests as far as possible, and to critically engage themselves intellectually, politically, and ethically. That said, Oberlin students can prepare for professional degrees in areas such as medicine, law, engineering, or architecture while also receiving a diverse education spanning the humanities, social sciences, and natural sciences. The majority of Oberlin students see their education as an opportunity to learn as much as they can in as many different areas as possible before continuing on to graduate school, or begin their careers.

Oberlin College is unique in many ways. It was the first college in the United States to accept minorities and women, it has never been home to a single fraternity or sorority, and it has one of the finest library and art collections in the nation. Also, since the College is adjacent to the internationally-accredited Conservatory of Music, students have the opportunity to hear world-class music on a regular basis, often without paying a cent. Students are guaranteed an academically-stimulating and personally-enriching experience at Oberlin, but they must also be prepared for an intense workload, small-town life, less than ideal weather, and four challenging years in a small community of students and faculty.

If you are thinking about going to Oberlin, you probably already have your own personal reasons for choosing it. No amount of facts or student testimonies will prepare you for the unique experiences you are bound to have there. Hopefully this book will give you some idea of what to expect and, more importantly, inspire you to find out more about Oberlin on your own terms. If one thing is certain about an Oberlin education it is that, in the words of educator and Oberlin alumnus Robert Maynard Hutchins, it will "unsettle the minds of the young and inflame their intellects." No matter what you expect, it's almost sure to be different.

Sarah LeBaron von Baeyer, Author
Oberlin College

By the Numbers

General Information

Oberlin College
173 W. Lorain St.
Oberlin, OH 44074

Control:
Private

Academic Calendar:
Semester

Religious Affiliation:
None

Founded:
1833

Web Site:
www.oberlin.edu

Main Phone:
(440) 775-8121

Admissions Phone:
(440) 775-8411
(800) 622-6243

Student Body

**Full-Time
Undergraduates:**
2,741

**Part-Time
Undergraduates:**
66

**Total Male
Undergraduates:**
1,267

**Total Females
Undergraduates:**
1,540

Admissions

Overall Acceptance Rate:
37%

Early Decision Acceptance Rate:
61%

Regular Acceptance Rate:
36%

Total Applicants:
6,236

Total Acceptances:
2,300

Freshman Enrollment:
742

Yield (% of admitted students who actually enroll):
31%

Early Decision Available?
Yes

Early Action Available?
No

Early Decision Deadline:
November 15

Early Decision Notification:
December 10

Regular Decision Deadline:
January 15

Regular Decision Notification:
April 1

Must-Reply-By Date:
May 1

Applicants Placed on Waiting List:
791

Applicants Accepted from Waiting List:
274

Students Enrolled From Waiting List:
63

Transfer Applications Received:
285

Transfer Applications Accepted:
94

Transfer Students Enrolled:
49

Transfer Applicant Acceptance Rate:
32%

Common Application Accepted?
Yes

Supplemental Forms?
Yes

Admissions E-Mail:
college.admissions@
oberlin.edu

➜

Admissions Web Site:
www.oberlin.edu/coladm

SAT I or ACT Required?
Either

**SAT I Range
(25th–75th Percentile):**
1250–1440

**SAT I Verbal Range
(25th–75th Percentile):**
640–730

**SAT I Math Range
(25th–75th Percentile):**
610–710

SAT II Requirements:
None (Although it is
recommended to take them)

Retention Rate:
91%

**Top 10% of
High School Class:**
68%

Application Fee:
$35

Financial Information

Tuition:
$32,724

Room and Board:
$8,180

Books and Supplies:
$762

**Average Need-Based
Financial Aid Package
(including loans, work-study,
grants, and other sources):**
$23,006

Financial Aid Forms Deadline:
January 15

**Students Who Applied for
Financial Aid:**
68%

Students Who Received Aid:
60%

Financial Aid Phone:
(440) 775-8142
(800) 693-3173

Financial Aid E-Mail:
financial.aid@oberlin.edu

Financial Aid Web Site:
www.oberlin.edu/finaid

Academics

The Lowdown On...
Academics

Degrees Awarded:
Bachelor
Post-Bachelor Certificate
Master

Most Popular Majors:
16% Music Performance
11% English
 9% Biology
 9% Political Science
 8% History

Undergraduate Schools:
College of Arts and Sciences
Conservatory of Music

Full-Time Faculty:
269

Faculty with Terminal Degree:
95%

➜

Student-to-Faculty Ratio:
10:1

Average Course Load:
Four classes

Graduation Rates:
Four-Year: 64%

Five-Year: 78%

Six-Year: 79%

Special Degree Options
3-2 Engineering program, Double-degree program of Bachelor of Arts and Bachelor of Music

AP Test Score Requirements
Possible credit for scores of 4 or 5

IB Test Score Requirements
Possible credit for scores of 6 or 7

Best Places to Study
Art Library, MUDD Library, and Science Center

Did You Know?

Oberlin provides a winter term of four weeks in January to encourage and enable students to discover the value of self-education. This term affords students an opportunity to devise and pursue programs of independent study or research. It also gives students the chance to undertake, individually or within a group, on or off campus, other projects of educational value that the structured curriculum during the academic year cannot accommodate easily. Oberlin presents its students with the chance to learn exactly what they want on their own terms.

The Experimental College (Exco) is a department of a non-traditional curriculum taught by students, townspeople, faculty, and staff. Absolutely anyone can take an Exco course, students can take Exco courses for credit, and up to five Exco credits can be applied towards graduation. If you ever wanted to learn Kiswahili, go sailing, or take a course in sexual health issues, this is the perfect opportunity to do so.

The Honor Committee is a student-run organization that is responsible for the continued health of the honor system at Oberlin. The purpose of the honor system is to maintain in Oberlin a high standard of academic integrity with respect to all curricular work.

Although the library has a large collection, students sometimes need publications and other materials that the library does not own. **Through Inter-Library Loan, students have access to materials from libraries all over the country**, and even the world. Even better, though, is OhioLINK, a free service available to students and faculty, which allows direct requests from academic libraries within Ohio. This means that students at Oberlin have quick and easy access to an incredible amount of scholarly works—perhaps one of the most important resources one could hope for at college.

→

In every department, there are **seminar classes reserved for freshmen**. These classes offer freshmen the opportunity to experience the exciting intellectual dynamic of small discussion groups with other first-year students and faculty. Freshmen seminars offer an excellent opportunity to forge close relationships with professors at the beginning of your academic career.

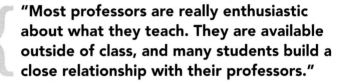

Students Speak Out On...
Academics

"Most professors are really enthusiastic about what they teach. They are available outside of class, and many students build a close relationship with their professors."

Q "I have found the teachers here at Oberlin to be **incredibly supportive**. If you have difficulties, they don't automatically send you to a TA or brush you off. They'll listen to you—listen to your problems, dreams, wishes— anything. They're simply available, which I think you don't find in a lot of major universities. I won't pretend that every professor I've had is a captivating lecturer, but the vast majority have been brilliant and enthusiastic, and truly love their subject."

Q "The **teachers at Oberlin are awesome**. They're extremely knowledgeable and passionate, and they take a strong interest in students' needs. Because the school is small, students can get to know their teachers well, and there tends to be a strong sense of community within departments."

Q "The teachers are extremely casual, but expect a lot out of their students. Though many classes take an informal tone, **the course work is often quite a load**. Occasionally, professors can seem unsympathetic to non-academic issues, but if you put in the effort to get to know a few, it can be quite rewarding."

Q "The majority of the **teachers are competent, and the classes are interesting**. However, some teachers are proficient at the subject they are teaching, but have a horrendous lack of ability to relate/interact with their students."

Q "I really liked some of my teachers, kind of liked some of my teachers, and was bored by some of my teachers. For the most part, I felt like classes were fairly interesting as long as the subject interested me, and my professors usually tried their best to keep the class lively. Sometimes, discussions were hampered by other kids in the class who tended towards being pompous and being overqualified nerds in the subject. But yeah, **professors are good, smart, and engaging**. There were a few in my four years who were totally amazing, and I had great relationships with them. There are some really brilliant scholars on campus."

Q "Both newly minted **PhDs and stalwarts of the various departments share one thing in common: passion**. In their in- and out-of-class demeanor, it's easy to see their commitment not only to their area of interest, but also to students and to teaching. 'Interesting' seems less apt an adjective than 'challenging,' 'engaging,' or 'extremely difficult.'"

Q "As with any other school, there are good classes and bad classes, and good teachers and bad teachers; though I'm generally happy with the class offerings. **You learn what to avoid** once you've been around a bit."

Q "**Teachers, overall, are great**. There are some departments that are better than others, for example, the Chinese/East Asian Studies department and the math department are both very good, whereas philosophy is only so-so."

Q "**Good professors** are spread out over lots of disciplines."

Q "Many professors are politically active and aware. **Some of my best professors were demagogues and ideologues**. Those were interesting classes, I'll tell you."

Q "**The teachers, from what I've experienced, are all amazing at their field**, incredible resources, and extremely intelligent. Occasionally, you'll find the professor who doesn't exactly mesh with your personality or learning style, but that's to be expected at any college."

Q "The quality of classes vary by teachers greatly; some **classes are extremely stimulating**, and others are dull."

Q "There are lots of flavors and personalities. **I've enjoyed most of my classes**, and nothing beats an excellent and inspiring teacher. They make you feel like studying more and more."

Q "**The professors are a quirky and interesting bunch**, which makes them easy to talk to and fun to watch in lectures, although 'quirky' can sometimes mean impossible to follow."

Q "Basically, the teachers rule, as a group. They care about what they're teaching, and that you learn it. Some have a tendency to run on during lectures, which can be boring, but on the whole, they're a quality staff. And yes, **the classes are, for the most part, interesting**."

The College Prowler Take On...
Academics

As is the case at any college, classes at Oberlin range from the life-altering to the barely-tolerable. The majority, however, are personally enriching and intellectually delightful. The choice of classes at Oberlin is extensive. Even if regular academics don't quite fit the bill, classes taught through the Experimental College program (Excos)—everything from '80s Movies to Chainmail & Calligraphy—surely will. In fact, there are so many choices of interesting classes to take at Oberlin that students sometimes feel frustrated there isn't enough time for everything. It isn't uncommon for students to take a maximum number of credit hours, not because they have to, but because they don't want to miss out on a really great class. Oberlin students are almost masochistic about having busy schedules, and consequently, a serious work ethic prevails on campus.

Without a doubt, one of the best things about classes at Oberlin is their size—the small-class environment leads to stimulating discussions and a more intimate rapport between students and professors. The discussion-intensive nature of most classes can be intimidating to students who are not already accustomed to speaking up in front of their peers, but most students are glad not to spend all their time in big lecture halls. Professors at Oberlin are also conspicuously passionate about teaching, and they encourage meeting individually with students. Some professors even invite entire classes over for a cook-out at their house and, if you're lucky, an additional lecture in romantic poetry. All in all, students at Oberlin have access to all the resources necessary—be it engaging professors, or the extensive library collection—to having a stimulating and gratifying academic experience.

The College Prowler® Grade on

Academics: A

A high Academics grade generally indicates that professors are knowledgeable, accessible, and genuinely interested in their students' welfare. Other determining factors include class size, how well professors communicate, and whether or not classes are engaging.

Local Atmosphere

The Lowdown On...
Local Atmosphere

Region:
Midwest

City, State:
Oberlin, Ohio

Setting:
Small town

Distance from Cleveland:
30 minutes

Points of Interest:
Allen Memorial Art Museum
The Arb
Chance Creek
The Firelands Association for the Visual Arts (FAVA)
Oberlin Heritage Center
Jones' Farm
The Kipton-Lorain Bike Trail
Martin Luther King Park
Tappan Square
The Olive and Scott Carson Nature Reserve
Welzheimer-Johnson House
Westwood Cemetery

Closest
Shopping Malls:

Great Northern Mall
4954 Great Northern Mall,
North Olmsted
(440) 734-6300\

Southpark Center
500 Southpark Center.,
Cleveland
(440) 238-9000

Westfield Shoppingtown
Midway Mall
3343 Midway Mall, Elyria
(440) 324 5749
http://westfield.com/midway

Closest
Movie Theaters:

The Apollo
19 East College Street, Oberlin
(440) 774-7091

Cleveland Cinema Cedar Lee
2163 Lee Road, Cleveland
(440) 717-4696

**(Closest Movie
Theaters, continued)**

The Cleveland Cinematheque
11141 East Boulevard,
Cleveland
(216) 421-7450

Regal Cinemas
5500 Cobblestone Road, Elyria
(440) 934-3356

Major Sports Teams:

Cleveland Barons (hockey)

Cleveland Browns (football)

Cleveland Cavaliers
(basketball)

Cleveland Indians (baseball)

Columbus Crew (soccer)

City Web Sites

www.oberlin.org
www.oberlinheritage.org
www.college360.org

Did You Know?

5 Fun Facts about Oberlin:

- Oberlin College was the **first interracial and coeducational college** in the United States.

- The first women in the United States to receive bachelor's degrees graduated from Oberlin in 1841. Later, in 1862, **Mary Jane Patterson** graduated from Oberlin—the first African American woman in the United States to receive a BA.

- **Oberlin was once a major stop on the Underground Railroad**. Today, you can see the Underground Railroad sculpture on South Professor Street, across from Oberlin College's Conservatory of Music. The railroad tracks that emerge from the ground were designed and installed by students.

- The **Allen Memorial Art Museum** was founded in 1917. The collection now contains more than 11,000 works of art that span history. It is the largest collection held by an undergraduate institution, and the third largest held by any educational institution after Harvard and Yale.

- **Aluminum was first extracted in Oberlin** in 1886 by Charles Martin Hall. Today, Oberlin still benefits from the money made by ALCOA.

Famous Clevelanders:

Halle Berry

Drew Carey

Hart Crane

James A. Garfield

Arsenio Hall

Charles Martin Hall

Margaret Hamilton

Dennis Kucinich

Paul Newman

Jesse Owens

Sam Sheppard

Students Speak Out On...
Local Atmosphere

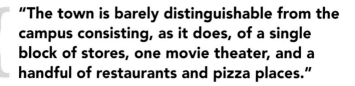

"The town is barely distinguishable from the campus consisting, as it does, of a single block of stores, one movie theater, and a handful of restaurants and pizza places."

Q "Oberlin is a small, small Ohio town. You can pretty much get everything in town, but it is usually overpriced. A good point is that there are many restaurants for this size of town. I mean, you don't get too bored in Oberlin since **there is always stuff going on**."

Q "**The town of Oberlin is pretty small**—no other universities. The college is one of the town's major employers. The Allen Memorial Art Museum is definitely a must-see. I highly recommend bringing a bike and checking out the bike trail that angles through town and out into the surrounding farmland."

Q "**Oberlin is a pretty typical college town** with the usual mix of restaurants, bookstores, and bars. The downtown is small, and right next to campus, so it's very easy to get coffee or go shopping. There also is an old movie theater with a big, old-fashioned marquee that plays late-run movies for a few dollars."

Q "Rural. Midwest. **Think cornfields in all directions**. Pleasant in some respects (no Wal-Mart or Starbucks in sight), but a pain in many others (off-campus nightlife is wishful thinking). The area is rich with small mom and pop stores, and restaurants, but one is blind to these options without serious transportation. Lake Erie does provide a nice change to the farmland monotony with its piddly waves and artificial beaches."

Q "Oberlin can best be described as a quaint, if somewhat small, rural town. Outside of the downtown area, there aren't many busy places. The best parts are definitely the quiet, secluded areas like the Arb, the bike trail, the tree/bench between Hall Auditorium and the Art building, and Tappan Square, the verdant park right off the center of campus. **The Apollo theater** on College Street is a popular attraction, as they play a second-run movie each week for three dollars a ticket (two dollars on Tuesdays and Thursdays). There's not really much to visit (though there is a Frank Lloyd Wright house), but there are nice places to relax."

Q "Town? I live in a town? Cool. **No other universities**. As far as stuff to stay away from, I know there is some public housing in the town, but it's not really a big deal, as far as I can see. See the Apollo; man, what a great movie theater."

Q "**I like Oberlin as a town**. Maybe the southwestern part of the residential area is slightly less desirable, but there's no reason to go there anyway. Ohio State is three hours away, Case Western Reserve is in Cleveland, and there's several schools in Akron."

Q "**Oberlin is very small and cozy** with a homey atmosphere."

Q "The town is the college in my opinion. **It's very small**, very quaint. One of the greatest places to visit is the Allen Memorial Art Museum. For a small, liberal art college, it packs quite the punch with works by Picasso, Monet, and Andy Warhol."

Q "Oberlin is surrounded by corn and soybean fields, and poorer, rural neighborhoods. Nonetheless, the campus has a lot of **exotic flowering trees** to brighten the mood of the students, and make them think they're in a tropical *Our Town*."

Q "Oberlin's a really small town and has **only one bar**. This means that you can't really avoid anyone, so you better not burn your bridges. But it's actually a pretty nice small town, and it's really worthwhile to seek activities that involve town residents (i.e. tutoring kids, working at town businesses, the Bike Co-op, community projects—check out the big parade that happens every year)."

Q "There are big universities in Akron and Cleveland, but students don't tend to visit them. Oberlin is surrounded by pretty and boring farmland, and **you should take advantage of the availability of cheap, fresh, local produce**. Oberlin itself is fairly diverse, in that the kids in the college are often wealthy and white (with many exceptions, and it has a significant population of people of color, but this is the national trend of who is going to college), and the town is primarily black and lower income."

Q "**Don't assume that you're always welcome on your neighbors turf**; do your best to be respectful and remember that some people live there year-round, and don't think your loud parties are awesome."

Q "I think the college is the biggest influence on the town itself. **You don't really run into people from other schools** (though both the Cleveland universities and Wooster are only about an hour away), and so the Oberlin-bubble feeling is pretty pervasive, especially if you don't try and interact with the town itself."

Q "Tiny town, and it's the only university around for at least an hour. **There isn't specific stuff to visit, since it's so small**, you end up going everywhere anyway, but there are definitely parts of town you want to avoid—some townies really dislike us."

The College Prowler Take On...
Local Atmosphere

Students often joke that Oberlin is situated in between two cornfields, affectionately referring to it as "the Harvard of the Midwest." While Oberlin is a typical small college town, its unique history and cultural assets lend it a distinctive air. Some of the best things about the town are its cozy, peaceful atmosphere, its numerous green areas, its quaint, old movie theater, and its thriving cultural scene. In terms of the arts and music, much of the cultural life in Oberlin is generated by the college and the conservatory, and students often spend more time on campus than they do in the surrounding neighborhoods. When they do manage to get off campus, students tend to make the 40-minute drive into Cleveland and take advantage of the free Art Museum, the Cedar Lee Theatre, excellent restaurants, and a general change of scene.

Despite the friendly vibe one gets walking into a small bank or shop in Oberlin, there is a noticeable divide between college students and locals. Oberlin's economy depends largely on the college, causing some town residents to feel resentful towards the ever-changing crowds of students who rarely become a permanent part of the local community. Even so, some students try and get involved with the local community through activities such as tutoring, part-time jobs, and even organic farming. Every spring, the Big Parade links town and gown in a fun and creative way, allowing students to mingle with children from the local public schools, and share in a diverse community of people of all ages.

The College Prowler® Grade on
Local Atmosphere: D+

A high Local Atmosphere grade indicates that the area surrounding campus is safe and scenic. Other factors include nearby attractions, proximity to other schools, and the town's attitude toward students.

Safety & Security

The Lowdown On...
Safety & Security

Number of Oberlin Police:

9

Oberlin Police Phone:

(440) 775-8911 (emergencies)

(440) 775-8444
(non-emergencies)

Safety Services:

Controlled dorm access

Crime prevention programs

Emergency blue-light telephones

Late-night shuttle/escort van

Self defense classes

Health Services:

Basic laboratory services

Gynecological health care

Some immunization

Treatment of common ailments

Student Health Center

247 West Lorain, Suite A

(440) 775-8180

Nurse Access Line: (800) 322-9679 (24 hours, 7 days per week)

www.oberlin.edu/health/services.htm

Monday, Wednesday, and Friday 8:30 a.m.–4:30 p.m.,
Tuesday and Thursday 10 a.m.–6 p.m.,
Saturday 10 a.m.–1 p.m.

Sexual Information Center

The SIC offers safer sex information from a student-run, non-profit organization. Because the SIC is run by college students, it offers the widest range of services a sex-ed organization could offer, ranging from counseling and discount safer-sex products, to alternative menstrual products and sex toys. The SIC also has a lending library on sexual health and offers free clinic rides to those who need them.

Wilder Student Union, Room 203

(440) 775-8135

Open daily 3 p.m.–6 p.m., and Monday–Thursday 8–10 p.m.

Did You Know?

Professor James Walsh, Professor of Sociology at Oberlin College, was **once also the District Attorney for the town of Oberlin**. So watch what you do in his courtroom!

One of the most serious crimes in recent times at Oberlin was when **a college student hoisted a heavy womb chair out of Mudd Library**, rappelled it over the roof of the building, and dragged the valuable piece of vintage furniture off campus. Unfortunately for him, the student was caught, and the college has since cracked down on womb chair theft.

Students Speak Out On...
Safety & Security

"I think security's adequate. I generally feel pretty safe. For people who are used to big cities, Oberlin's a breath of fresh air. The campus security squad is usually pretty reasonable and helpful."

Q "**People walk alone on campus at two in the morning**, and there is no problem. There is a bus nicknamed the 'drunk bus' that takes people from place to place, in case you feel unsafe on campus or are too inebriated to drive."

Q "I have **always felt safe** on campus."

Q "I haven't had too many encounters with Oberlin's police. **They seem pretty cool**, though. There's one really fat dude who's always smoking a pipe."

Q "Safety and security people can be notoriously difficult to deal with, but for the most part, **the campus is pretty safe**. The streets are relatively safe at night, and except for laptops stolen from libraries and the like, things are secure as long as you're careful."

Q "We rarely locked our house door all year. Security is inept. Their most important jobs, though, are locking building doors and writing parking tickets that aren't strictly enforced. **Rarely do I think twice about Oberlin being remotely unsafe**."

Q "Safety and security is okay, but **students sometimes sneak into dorms** when another student swipes their IDs—this is called tailgating into the dorms."

Q "**I feel generally safe** walking around the campus, even at night, but I don't know if I'm being overconfident. The college safety and security are pretty much what I'd expected."

Q "Safety and security is pretty cool. **They don't like busting people or breaking up parties**, they'd rather come in and help fix things, but they will do their jobs!"

Q "**It's very safe**. Many cops and security guards are around late at night, too."

Q "As a girl, I walk alone at two in the morning sometimes; **it's really quite safe**."

Q "My only experience with campus safety comes from climbing up onto the roofs of various Oberlin College buildings. **They seemed pretty chill** when I met them, though."

Q "I've never had a problem where I needed to call security, so I would say **safety and security is pretty good**."

Q "Occasionally, a laptop or a bicycle is stolen, but **people often leave their doors unlocked**. All the security guys are super hot, and I want to marry them all!"

Q "**Generally, the campus feels very safe**. Most paths and streets are well lit, there are over 60 emergency phone booths spread all over campus, and if you're still not feeling safe, you can take a free shuttle back to your dorm or house. I'm female, and I walk across campus alone at night all the time without feeling the least bit insecure."

The College Prowler Take On...
Safety & Security

Perhaps because Oberlin is such a small town, people tend to take for granted that serious crimes rarely ever happen. Still, the College's Office of Safety and Security has done everything possible to ensure that the campus is extremely safe. Emergency phones are attached to blue-light posts all around campus, and the Student Shuttle System allows students who feel either unsafe to walk or too inebriated to drive from running into trouble. Most female students admit to feeling very safe when they walk across campus late at night, especially because all paths and streets tend to be well lit, and clear of huge bushes or trees. All dorms require ID cards to enter, and as a result, many students don't always feel the need to lock their doors.

One of the main problems that occurs on campus is theft, mostly in places like Mudd Library or Wilder Bowl, where students often leave their belongings unattended for long periods of time. Safety and Security officers generally do a very good job of tracking down stolen items and, for the most part, students tend not to steal from other students. Even so, Safety and security encourages students to register their bicycles with the school in case they are stolen, and then turn up a week later in the town creek—as has been known to happen before.

A-

The College Prowler® Grade on
Safety & Security: A-

A high grade in Safety & Security means that students generally feel safe, campus police are visible, blue-light phones and escort services are readily available, and safety precautions are not overly necessary.

Computers

The Lowdown On...
Computers

High-Speed Network?
Yes

Number of Computers:
276

Wireless Network?
Yes

Operating Systems:
Mac, PC, UNIX

Number of Labs:
21

Free Software

Adobe Reader, Mathmatica, McAfee virus software, Mulberry e-mail, Novell Client, SPSS and other stat programs, Photoshop, and various browsers

Discounted Software

Adobe Creative Suite, Dream Weaver MX, Microsoft Office, Norton System Works

24-Hour Labs

Burton, Kade, and Lord Saunders

Charge to Print?

Yes, 7 cents per sheet, and 9 cents per duplex (after $10.50 quota is used up, which usually equals around 150–233 free pages).

Did You Know?

Oberlin College has its own computer store in the MUDD building where students can purchase Gateway, Apple, and sometimes various types of used computers.

Computers

"During finals and midterm exams, computer labs are crowded. Oberlin is working on making more lab space available, but it is really nice to have your own computer."

Q "I think **it's definitely a good idea to bring your own computer** since all the dorm rooms are connected to the Internet. Labs are not that crowded, but during exam periods, they can be really crowded."

Q "**Definitely bring your own computer**. The network has occasional bugs, and randomly went down for a week or so right before exams one year, causing some healthy panic, but normally, it is fairly reliable. The administration has decided to close one of the larger computer labs this year, so 24-hour lab access is something of a question right now."

Q "You should bring your own computer wherever you go to school. **There are lots of computer labs at Oberlin**, and they're often crowded. The network can be slow sometimes, but they're working on it, or so they say."

Q "Educational pricing. If you can afford a computer, take advantage of the fact that manufacturers knock down prices for students. Otherwise, I wouldn't say a computer is 'necessary;' having one is a luxury, but lacking a box is not a problem either. **Computer network is decent**; all you'll use it for is AIM, Friendster, e-mail, and downloading music anyway. Labs get crowded around midterms and finals, but if one is resourceful, this needn't be a problem."

Q "You get **occasional problems with the network**, but I haven't had a real problem with it. It would probably be helpful to have your own computer, especially since we lost Briggs Lab. If I need one, I can generally find an open computer in Mudd or the science center, except for maybe around midterms and finals."

Q "If you have one, bring one. The **main lab in the library tends to be pretty crowded** during finals. There are a bunch of other labs, and you don't need a computer, but it is helpful."

Q "Bring a computer—**it's always crowded** (especially near finals), plus it's just more convenient."

Q "There are **four major computer labs on campus**, none of which are regularly filled. Access to a public computer only becomes difficult around finals or midterms. Bringing your own computer is convenient, but not necessary."

Q "The computer labs can get crowded. I have a computer at school and, for most part, it is the norm among students, but that doesn't mean it has to be. **The network was incredibly slow** this past semester, but otherwise, the school does a very good job of keeping the software and computers up-to-date."

Q "**It's convenient to have one's own computer**. I personally call it a necessity, but I don't see anyone feeling handicapped without one—it's just that you may need to spend considerable amounts of time outside your dorm room in one of the public labs, and if you're lazy like me, you may have to have a little discipline not to burn the midnight oil."

Q "Having your own computer is definitely nice, but not necessary. Some computer labs are always packed (especially around finals), but there is usually somewhere to print or whatever you need. **The network is up and down**, but mostly dependable."

Q "**Bring a computer** if you have the means, but there are computer labs, and one rarely has to wait to use a station."

Q "The computer labs, especially on A-level of Mudd Library, are often pretty full, but the network, despite occasional slowness, is actually pretty good. With everything online, from grades to class registration, to a plethora of class and extra-curricular e-mails, **a computer is definitely worth the price**."

Q "The computer network is good. Computer labs get crowded at and near exam period. **It is helpful to bring a computer**, although not necessary."

The College Prowler Take On...
Computers

Computers are an absolute necessity at Oberlin. Ideally, you should have your own computer so you don't have to bother with all the noise and activity of the computer labs. Even for those who can't afford one, there are enough computers on campus to satisfy everyone's needs. The only time you have to worry about finding an available computer in the labs is around exam period, when everyone frantically tries to print out articles and type up essays all at the same time. For students who live on campus, all dorm rooms are supplied with unlimited Internet access—an important asset, considering everything from class registration to communication with professors is done online. Also worth noting is the fact that at Mudd Library, you can borrow a laptop free of charge.

With three computer labs opened 24 hours a day, students can use the computers situated in the basement of Burton, Kade, and Lord Saunders until the wee hours of the morning. The Computer Store, located on the A-Level of Mudd, offers significant discounts for students and is a good option for students looking to buy a computer once they get to Oberlin. Most dorms have their own RCCs—students who specialize in computers, and are available to help people with whatever computer-related problems they might encounter. The college employs RCCs so that students don't have to pay anything themselves; all they have to do is send an e-mail to their nearest RCC, and help will be on its way.

The College Prowler® Grade on

Computers: B+

A high grade in Computers designates that computer labs are available, the computer network is easily accessible, and the campus' computing technology is up-to-date.

Facilities

The Lowdown On...
Facilities

Student Center:
Wilder Hall

Athletic Center:
Jesse Philips Physical
Education Center

John W. Heisman Field House

Libraries:
4

Popular Places to Chill:
The Arboretum
Decafé
Tappan Square
Wilder Bowl

Campus Size:
440 acres

What Is There to Do on Campus?

In between classes, you can join a protest, go for a bike ride, grab a bite to eat at Decafé, watch a game of Frisbee in Wilder Bowl, hear students practice in the Conservatory, take in a play, meander around the Allen Memorial Art Museum, or attend one of many stimulating lectures by visiting scholars, artists, and activists without ever leaving the school campus.

Movie Theater on Campus?

Not officially, but there are often movie viewings all over campus, and the Apollo Theater is just down the street.

Bowling on Campus?

Yes, the College Lanes at 180 West Lorain Street.

Bar on Campus?

Yes, the Dionysus Club, (known as the 'Sco by students) is a discotheque located in the basement of Wilder Student Union which serves both alcoholic and non-alcoholic drinks.

Coffeehouse on Campus?

Yes, the Cat in the Cream, located in Hales Annex, at 180 West Lorain Street.

Favorite Things to Do

Guest lectures usually draw a larger audience than any sports events do, and students flock to Craig Lecture Hall, King, Peters, Wilder Hall, and the Environmental Studies Center to imbue themselves with the words of wisdom of visiting scholars, writers, and political activists. Because Oberlin also has a Conservatory of Music, the school draws renowned musicians from around the world, and students often line up in front of Finney Chapel or the 'Sco to hear anything from classical music concerts to punk rock shows—all for only a few dollars. The Cat in the Cream offers student sketch comedy, solo poetry readings, and musical performances. For less intellectual stimulation, the on-campus bowling allies provide ample time to relax and hit the pins, or just gaze at the stars and contemplate the universe in the Peters Observatory.

Students Speak Out On...
Facilities

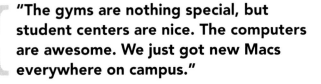

"The gyms are nothing special, but student centers are nice. The computers are awesome. We just got new Macs everywhere on campus."

Q "Phillips Gym, the main athletic facility, is fairly nice. There is extensive weight and cardiovascular equipment, as well as more esoteric stuff, like a climbing wall, a fencing room with armory, and many squash and racquetball courts. A small, but fairly nice **indoor-track and tennis-court area** is also a part of the gym. I don't spend much time in the computer labs. The student center, Wilder Hall, is due for renovation soon, but is still pretty great. It's old, but you can easily get rooms for study groups or small rehearsals, and it houses many clubs and activities—from a meditation room to the campus radio station."

Q "The facilities that matter for getting a good education are awesome. The libraries are huge and nicely designed, and the labs and studio spaces are great, but the gym and the dorms aren't exactly posh. You'll never think you're at a country club when you're at Oberlin, but you'll have **the best facilities available for learning** what you came to college to learn."

Q "Computers are pretty well-kept on campus, as well as quite current. The athletics building is nice, and offers an indoor running track, tennis courts (almost always occupied by teams), racquetball courts, a swimming pool, and various exercise equipment. **The library is one of the best in the country** and has pretty much anything you need."

Q "Athletic: for a Division III school of our size, **we have sweet facilities**. Computers: no complaints; CIT seems to have hardware and software up to date. Student Center: we get great concerts, the 'Sco is cheap; Wilder is great."

Q "Facilities are fine—there's a great **new science building and a nice science library**. The humanities students study in the science library because it's quiet and comfortable. I don't know much about athletic facilities. The computers are fine. Kids are revving for another student theater space, but budgetary challenges are preventing them from getting anywhere. As for the dorms, they're fairly average, I think."

Q "**The gym isn't really great**—you usually have to sign up in advance if you want to use one of the popular machines, but there's usually something available (if you don't mind using the weird retro stationary bikes, anyway)."

Q "Overall, facilities are pretty nice. **There is a nice, big gym** for all sorts of athletic stuff."

Q "**The facilities are nice, and not overcrowded**. The gymnasium space is often open for casual athletics, and decent equipment is available without charge or need of an appointment. There is a lack of theater space, and many student drama groups are peeved about this. There's no political space for the disadvantaged students, but there's nothing new about that."

Q "I don't know much about the athletic facilities except that they suit my needs; they function. **We need a better student theater**, but the student union is a great resource for clubs and people. The libraries are also great. Besides the beautiful womb chairs, the science library and the art library are both great places to study if you're not into '70s-foam decor."

Q "Facilities on campus are nice. Not superb, but **we have all the necessaries**. It's entirely up to the student whether to take advantage of this or not."

Q "Oberlin has one of the best libraries and **best art collections in the country**. What more are you looking for?"

Q "I think the facilities are all very good, though I'm not athletic. **The computers are all quite new, and pretty fast**."

Q "The facilities meet their purposes pretty well. **The gym and the computer labs are pretty standard**, and pretty nice. The student union is too small to hold the big events comfortably, which makes it charming."

Q "Phillips is a great gym—the teams aren't quite as hot, but hey, this is Oberlin; that's not why want to you come, is it? The **buildings are clean** and don't usually smell (except dorms on weekends; that's not the college's fault, it's the students')."

Q "The student center, science center, and athletic center are **all nice**!"

The College Prowler Take On...
Facilities

At Oberlin, the facilities necessary for a good education are first rate. Oberlin's library collection of books and periodicals, scores, government publications, sound and video recordings, and software contains over two million separate items. In addition, the library has access to a strong and growing collection of online resources. The Allen Memorial Art Museum is a favorite amongst students—its vast collection of interesting art from around the world is, amongst other undergraduate institutions, one of the finest in the country. The newly-built science center is spacious and well lit, and the Environmental Studies Building is a cutting-edge experiment in a green building. Even though Oberlin isn't renowned for its athletics, it does have all the perks of a major university, including a large swimming pool, personal training programs, and a football stadium. Don't forget about the incredible musical facilities of the Conservatory.

Despite the first-class facilities at Oberlin, buildings are not overly imposing or pretentious. Students tend to gather in Wilder Hall, the student union building—a cozy space with couches, TVs, gender-neutral bathrooms, and a snack bar, Decafé, downstairs. Wilder Hall is also home to the WOBC radio station, which houses an extensive collection of music, and is the pride and joy of many students involved in radio. Other excellent facilities include the Peters Observatory, Finney Chapel (for concerts and speeches), and the numerous all-Mac computer labs scattered around campus.

B+

The College Prowler® Grade on

Facilities: B+

A high Facilities grade indicates that the campus is aesthetically pleasing and well-maintained; facilities are state-of-the-art, and libraries are exceptional. Other determining factors include the quality of both athletic and student centers and an abundance of things to do on campus.

Campus Dining

The Lowdown On...
Campus Dining

Freshman Meal Plan Requirement?

Yes

Meal Plan Average Cost:

$1,950 (average plan available for freshmen)

$1,930–$1,400 (average plan available for upperclassmen)

$1,212 (co-ops)

Places to Grab a Bite with Your Meal Plan:

Coffee Kiosk

Food: Coffee, snacks

Location: Science center

Hours: Monday–Friday 7:30 a.m.–11 a.m., 11:30 a.m.–1:30 p.m.

Dascomb Food Court

Food: Deli, grill, International, pizza, salad bar, dessert bar

Location: West College Street (inside Dascomb Hall)

Hours: Monday–Friday 7:30 a.m.–2 p.m.

Sunday–Thursday 5 p.m.–8 p.m., 8:30 p.m.–11:30 p.m.

Lord Saunders

Food: All-you-can-eat, comfort food

Location: Forest Street (inside Afrikan Heritage House)

Hours: Sunday–Thursday 5:30 p.m.–7 p.m., yet during the second week of the month, Friday it is open from 5:30 p.m.–7 p.m.

Stevenson Dining Hall

Food: Pizza, deli, soups, grill, vegetarian

Location: North Professor Street

Hours: Monday–Sunday 11:30 a.m.–1:30 p.m., 5 p.m.–7:30 p.m., Saturday–Sunday 9 a.m.–11:15 a.m.

Wilder Decafé

Food: Snacks, sandwiches, salads

Location: West Lorain Street (Inside Wilder Hall)

Hours: Monday–Friday 9 a.m.–1 a.m., Saturday–Sunday 12 p.m.–12 a.m.

Wilder Rathskeller

Food: Buffet, á la carte

Location: Basement of Wilder Hall

Hours: Monday–Friday 11:45 a.m.–1:15 p.m.

Off-Campus Places to Use Your Meal Plan:
None

24-Hour On-Campus Eating?
No

Student Favorites:
Coffee Kiosk
Lord Saunders
Wilder Decafé

Other Options

Although students don't have a wide variety of dining options to choose from, they can use CDS Flex and Obie Dollars to buy food on and off campus. CDS Flex is a declining balance account built into the ID card, and may be used to purchase food from Decafé, or additional meals at any of the four CDS dining facilities. Obie Dollars are also available through a declining balance that students voluntarily purchase in advance and may use at select stores and restaurants off campus. For a special treat, Cookies on Call delivers freshly-baked cookies and cold milk late at night, when you are craving a study break, or an extra party snack. Students who live in the Third World House also have all the amenities to cook in their dorm.

Did You Know?

Oberlin's first co-op, Pyle Inn, was established in 1950 in response to **student's desire for more economical dining options**, and improved quality of service. Run by the Oberlin Student Cooperative Association (OSCA), co-ops are an excellent alternative to Campus Dining Services (CDS). Co-ops tend to offer more organic and vegetarian options and rely entirely upon the cooking abilities of their members. About 20 percent of Oberlin students choose co-ops over CDS.

Since the director of George Jones Memorial Farm, Brad Masi (Class of '93), worked with fellow students to redirect college dining into Northeastern Ohio, **Oberlin College's dining service now spends around $225,000** of a $2.84 million annual food budget locally.

The "Thinking of You" program allows relatives and friends to **send Oberlin students care packages** that will brighten their day, or lighten their late-night study sessions. Parents receive an order form in the mail shortly before the beginning of the school year and can pick from a number of different care packages, including ones for vegans and vegetarians!

Students Speak Out On...
Campus Dining

"Dining halls are sufficient, although most students dine less as they move up in class. Maybe a good idea to point out is the co-ops where students have more freedom to choose what and how to eat."

Q "Everybody will complain about campus food anywhere, but I think that **Campus Dining Services (CDS) at Oberlin does a fairly good job**. The main dining hall, Stevenson, has multiple vegetarian and vegan options, and often uses locally-grown produce, and makes an effort to supply fairly nutritional options, in addition to an 'everything fried' line. One of the big perks, for me, is that a local organic dairy supplies the milk. Stevenson is supplemented by a take-out dining hall, Dascomb, and a 'down home Southern-cooking' dining hall, Lord Saunders. The food at Dascomb does not usually compare to the other two."

Q "**Dining halls suck**, no matter where you go. That's all I have to say."

Q "The food in the dining halls is unremarkable. It's the **same kind of dining hall food that I've had at every college** I've ever been to, but they claim a lot of it is organic, or something like that. Fortunately, the co-ops save Oberlin students from culinary mediocrity. The ingredients are fresher, and the meals more creative, so the food is always much better. That is, as long as the people cooking that night know what they're doing."

Q "**Dining halls are decent**; I don't like the co-ops. Most will tell you the co-ops are better, but I can't stand them."

Q "Food is consistent in the dining halls—consistently sub-par. Things are getting better, but **Stevenson and Dascomb are consistent**; that's about it. Afrikan Heritage House is where it's at; north campus kids: it may seem far, but it's worth the hike. Co-ops are great when they're great, and crap when they serve beans and tofu delight. Inconsistent, but occasionally stellar; it's always a surprise."

Q "I never ate much in the dining halls; I ate in the **student cooperative system**, which is really fun, and I highly recommend it. There are eight student co-ops, including one for Kosher/Halal rules, and one called Third World that's geared towards people of color, and they run independently from the college. At Third World, students cook and clean all their meals in shifts—each member has to do about four hours of work a week, and it's about $1,000 cheaper than the other campus dining option. And the food is generally pretty healthy; lots of local produce and vegetarian cuisine, although there's meat too, that's usually nutritious and tasty, depending on the cook that night."

Q "The food on campus is average, institutional food. There are about five to six entreé options in each of the two main dining halls. One of Oberlin's main selling points is the Oberlin Student Cooperative Association (OSCA), an entirely student-run alternative to campus dining services. OSCA is 50 years old, and includes eight dining co-ops, and four housing co-ops, servicing 630 students. The co-opers are not all heady, nor are they all Jewish— except in Harkness and Fairchild. **The food in OSCA is consistently better than at the dining halls**, and sometimes, exceptional."

Q "**Eat at a co-op**. It's cheaper, friendlier, and the food is so much better. Oberlin College is known for really great co-ops."

Q "**The dining halls have lots of options**, but you get tired of any dining hall after a semester."

Q "There is always something edible to be found. The dining halls have **a pretty wide selection**, and even people with strange diets will not starve. There is not much choice eating in a co-op, but it's usually good food, and even mushy."

Q "Ugh. Food here is a pet peeve of mine. It's really good for the first three weeks, and you don't complain, but after three months of exactly the same stuff every day, it sucks. And **it's hard to eat healthy**, although it's pretty easy to eat vegetarian; not so much if you're vegan. For all non-meat eaters, I'd probably recommend a co-op, which are supposed to be pretty good, but are, in my experience, often hit-or-miss, and sometimes, kind of bland."

Q "**I prefer OSCA to CDS any day**—it's a good option, especially for the vegan/vegetarian/healthy food preferences. There may be some bad meals, but the good food can be really good. (CDS is always just mediocre at best, in my opinion.) At least you know where it came from with OSCA."

Q "**It all sucks**."

Q "The dining halls are okay. Food is average; it kind of **encourages people to eat mass quantities** because there's so much there, and then you feel gross afterwards."

The College Prowler Take On...
Campus Dining

Campus dining is never a treat exactly, but Oberlin does make a point of offering a wide selection of options for students with varying culinary preferences. All three dining halls, Dascomb, Stevenson, and Lord Saunders, include salad bars, fresh fruit, vegetarian, and fried-food options, as well as cereals and all the ingredients necessary for making sandwiches. Students often complain that the dining hall menus grow repetitive as the semester wears on, and that the food isn't seasoned with much flavor or pizzazz. Still, for dining hall food, it could be much worse than it is. At least students have the option of drinking local, organic milk, and munching on hummus and pita bread if they don't feel inclined towards the meat and potatoes baked in caramelized sugar.

Aside from Campus Dining Services (CDS), Oberlin offers an excellent alternative for students who prefer to cook their own food, work communally, and eat healthier: the co-ops. Co-ops are run by the Oberlin Student Cooperative Association, and are entirely managed by students. It is cheaper to join a co-op than to eat at CDS, but co-ops do have their downsides. First, you must be prepared to eat at exactly the same time every day, or you run the risk of missing out on all the food. Also, students in co-ops must put a certain number of hours into cooking and cleaning in the co-op every week, so if your schedule is overly busy, CDS might be the more efficient route. In general, even though some students complain co-ops are messy and disorganized, they are a healthier, cheaper, and more self-sufficient means of eating.

The College Prowler® Grade on
Campus Dining: C+

Our grade on Campus Dining addresses the quality of both school-owned dining halls and independent on-campus restaurants as well as the price, availability, and variety of food.

Off-Campus Dining

The Lowdown On...
Off-Campus Dining

Restaurant Prowler:
Popular Places to Eat!

Agave Burrito Bar and Tequilleria

Food: Mexican

19 West College St., Oberlin

(440) 774-7336

Price: $6–$10 per person

Hours: Monday–Thursday
11:30 a.m.–9 p.m., Friday–
Saturday 11:30 a.m.–11 p.m.,
Closed Sunday

Black River Café

Food: Breakfast, lunch

15 South Main St., Oberlin

(440) 775-3663

Price: $6–$10 per person

Special Features: Vegetarian
and organic options

Hours: Monday–Friday
8 a.m.–3 p.m., Saturday–Sunday
9 a.m.–3 p.m.

Downtown Pizza

Food: Pizza

38 South Main St., Oberlin

(440) 774-3700

(Downtown Pizza, continued)

Cool Features: Free delivery

Price: $5–$10 per person

Hours: Monday–Thursday
11 a.m.–2 a.m., Friday–
Saturday 11a.m.–2:30 a.m.,
Sunday 4 p.m.–1 a.m.

East of Chicago Pizza

Food: Pizza, wings, subs, pasta

175 South Main St., Oberlin

(440) 774-8820

www.eastofchicago.com

Price: $5–$10 per person

Hours: Monday–Saturday
11 a.m.–11 p.m., Sunday
12 p.m.–10 p.m.

Feve Coffeehouse & Deli

Food: Deli, coffeehouse

30 South Main St., Oberlin

(440) 774-1978

www.thefeve.com

Price: $4–$7 per person

Cool Features: Full bar

Hours: Monday–Sunday
11 a.m.–2 a.m., Saturday–
Sunday brunch 9:30 a.m.–
3 p.m.

Java Zone Café

Food: Hummus, wraps,
falafel, bagels

5 West College St.

(440) 774-5282

Price: $2–$9 per person

Hours: Monday–Thursday
7:30 a.m.–9 p.m.,
Friday 7:30 a.m.–10 p.m.,
Saturday 8 p.m.–10 p.m.,
Sunday 8 a.m.–9 p.m.

Lorenzo's Pizzeria

Food: American

52 ½ South Main St., Oberlin

(440) 775-0118

www.lorenzospizza.com

Price: $6–$16 per person

Hours: Monday–Thursday
11 a.m.–11 p.m., Friday–
Saturday 11 a.m.–12 a.m.,
Sunday 11:30 a.m.–11 p.m.

The Mandarin Chinese Restaurant

Food: Chinese

86 South Main St., Oberlin

(440) 774-4500

Cool Features: Lunch special
Sunday–Saturday 11:30 a.m.–
3 p.m.

Price: $8–$16 per person

Hours: Monday–Thursday
11:30 a.m.–9:30 p.m., Friday–
Saturday 11:30 a.m.–
10:30 p.m., Sunday
12 p.m.–9:30 p.m.

The Oberlin Market

Food: Healthy, organic, vegan

22 Carpenter Ct., Oberlin
(Behind the Feve)

(440) 774-8401

Price: $6–$10 per person

Hours: Monday–Friday
8:30 a.m.–7 p.m., Saturday
9 a.m.–5 p.m., Sunday
12 p.m.–5 p.m.

Subway

Food: Subs, salads
18 South Main St., Oberlin
(440) 774-7827
www.subway.com
Price: $6–$9 per person
Hours: Daily 8 a.m.–10 p.m.

Tooo Chinoise

Food: Chinese
27 West College St., Oberlin
(440) 774-2988
Price: $6–$15 per person
Hours: Daily 11:30 a.m.–
9:45 p.m.

Weia Teia

Food: Asian fusion, vegetarian
9 South Main St., Oberlin
(440) 774-8880
Cool Features: Discount menu
for lunch
Price: $16–$25 per person
Hours: Daily 11:30 a.m.–
9:30 p.m.

Student Favorites:

Black River Café
Feve Coffeehouse & Deli
Lorenzo's Pizzeria
Weia Teia

Other Places to Check Out:

Ben & Jerry's
Café Tandoor
Don Tequila Bar & Grill
Lola Bistro & Wine Bar
Seoul Hot Pot
Sergio's in University Circle
Woo City Ice Cream Co.

Late-Night, Half-Price Food Specials:

Feve Coffeehouse & Deli
The Mandarin Chinese
Restaurant
Weia Teia

24-Hour Eating:

No

Closest Grocery Stores:

Gibson's Food Mart
& Bakery
23 West College St., Oberlin
(440) 774-2401

Missler's Super Valu
291 South Main St., Oberlin
(440) 774-6205

Best Pizza:

Lorenzo's Pizzeria

Best Chinese:

Tooo Chinoise

Best Breakfast:

Black River Café

Best Wings:

The Feve Coffeehouse & Deli

Best Healthy:

The Oberlin Market

Best Place to Take Your Parents:

Weia Teia

Did You Know?

Jerry Greenfield (class of '73), is the **co-founder of Ben and Jerry's ice cream**; no matter where you go in Oberlin, you're sure to savor some of Jerry's success. If Ben and Jerry's isn't your thing, try the excellent flavors of Woo City, a local organic ice cream company.

Curly Tail Farms and Ohio Proud Hormone Free Meats provide restaurants like Black River Café with meat from farm-raised, hormone-free animals.

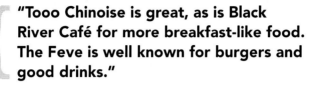

"Tooo Chinoise is great, as is Black River Café for more breakfast-like food. The Feve is well known for burgers and good drinks."

Q "Restaurants off campus **run the gamut**. There's Weia Teia, an Asian fusion place that most students consider to be on the expensive side, but worth the occasional splurge. In the Asian-food category, there's also Tooo Chinoise, a mediocre-to-good Chinese place, depending on what you order, and the Mandarin, which has a really good dish called Taste of Nirvana (seitan in sauce), but also attempts to do sushi a little too far from the coast. Black River Café is a must for breakfast; their omelets are to die for, and they do a decent never-ending-cup of coffee. Java Zone is the only other breakfast place; it has good scones, and little else of value. If you have a car, there's an expensive-but-good Italian place right outside of town. And of course, there are three or so pizza places of varying quality—the best being Lorenzo's."

Q "There aren't very many, and they're dominated by pan-Asian cuisine—**three different restaurants**! Weia Teia is the nicest place in town, and also the most expensive—lunches around seven or nine dollars, and dinners twice that. The Black River Café has good sandwiches, and great breakfast food for around six dollars. Java Zone has Mediterranean food, and isn't that great, but is pretty cheap. Then there's an assortment of bad pizza available, but then again, I'm from Chicago, and I am a pizza snob."

Q "We have a lot of **generic Asian restaurants that are pretty decent**—Weia Teia is probably the best. Black River Café is great for breakfast."

Q "There are many restaurants, and they are pretty decent. Let me tell you the hot spot: it's **the Java Zone**. Initially, this just looks like an average place to drink coffee, but it actually is really nice. You can people watch from the window, and easily pass a couple of hours in this way. Just stay away from the Mandarin."

Q "Oberlin has a great mix of restaurants for a town its size. **The Black River Café is definitely the best** place in town, considering food, price, and atmosphere, but it's only open for breakfast and lunch. The Feve has the best burgers in town, plus good wraps and hummus, and plenty of beer. Weia Teia is the place to go when your parents are footing the bill; the food is a creative Asian fusion, and the décor makes you think you're in Manhattan."

Q "There isn't much within walking distance, but a few places are actually pretty good. **Weia Teia is exorbitantly expensive, but is generally regarded as the haute cuisine**. Tooo Chinoise has a pretty good selection for the college student. Lorenzo's Pizzeria is my favorite place, and it's definitely classier than (if not open as late as) Downtown Pizza, which serves it by the slice."

Q "There is a decent selection of restaurants in town, although no 24-hour joint yet—and I've got beef with that. What's a college town with no 24-hour diner? Anyway, **Weia Teia if you want to eat really well**, Lorenzo's if you want pizza, Downtown Pizza if you're drunk and it's Saturday night, and the Mandarin or Tooo Chinoise if you're looking for a night out that doesn't break the bank."

Q "Oberlin has something like five restaurants in town. After the first two months, you'll know all of them. Try them all at least once; each has something interesting and distinctive to offer. After four years, though, you'll be sick of them (except **Black River, which has the best breakfasts around**)."

Q "Weia Teia is good, but expensive. **The Feve is always good**."

Q "Weia Teia is nice, yet funky. The Mandarin is acceptable, but not special. The burrito bar is fine; the chipotle sauce is especially good there. **The Feve serves quality pub grub**."

Q "There are **very few restaurants off campus** within the town: Weia Teia, Mandarin, Black River Café, Java Zone, Lorenzo's, and the Feve."

Q "There are **a handful of pizza places**, the Feve for burgers, a number of Asian-style places, and Black River Café for breakfast. The food is pretty good and, although there isn't much selection, it's often enough."

Q "Good places in town: **the Mandarin, and the Feve** (if you can deal with the service). Also, nearby in Amherst, is Don Tequila's, which is really good."

The College Prowler Take On...
Off-Campus Dining

For a town of its size, Oberlin offers a fair variety of restaurants, most of them specializing in Chinese/Asian and Mediterranean cuisine. Students from New York City are the most likely to complain about the choices, but if you don't mind making the drive to Cleveland, there's a larger selection to choose from, including excellent Indian food at Café Tandoor, and spicy Korean dishes at Seoul Hot Pot. As for Oberlin, if you ask anyone what his or her favorite restaurant is, most will tell you Black River Café. Black River serves only breakfast and lunch, but is extremely popular with students and faculty, especially on weekends, when it's best to arrive before 11 a.m. in order to avoid the long line-ups.

Although there isn't any 24-hour eating in town—a fact that aggravates many night-owls at Oberlin—there are a number of restaurants that keep their kitchens open until relatively late, including Downtown Pizza and the Feve. Most students enjoy the food at Weia Teia, but find it rather steep in price—the best deal is to go for lunch, when all main courses are much cheaper. The recently opened Agave is owned by the same people who run Black River Café, and is equally as delicious if you enjoy a healthy meal of burritos and tequila. Tooo Chinoise, the Mandarin, and Java Zone are common places to take a date, but if you're looking for a little more anonymity and chic décor, try Lola's Bistro or Sergio's in Cleveland.

The College Prowler® Grade on

Off-Campus Dining: B

A high Off-Campus Dining grade implies that off-campus restaurants are affordable, accessible, and worth visiting. Other factors include the variety of cuisine and the availability of alternative options (vegetarian, vegan, Kosher, etc.).

Campus Housing

The Lowdown On...
Campus Housing

Best Dorms:
East
Quadrangle (Asia House)
Talcott

Worst Dorms:
Dascomb
North

Undergrads Living on Campus:
75%

Number of Dormitories:
26

Number of University-Owned Apartments:
10 areas (all are off campus and reserved for upperclassmen)

→

Dormitories:

15 North Cedar Street

Floors: 2

Total Occupancy: 4

Bathrooms: Shared by apartment

Coed: Yes

Residents: Upperclassmen

Room Types: Four single bedrooms in one apartment

Special Features: Private bathrooms and kitchenettes, telephone and network connection, one couch, two living room chairs, a kitchen table with four chairs, smoking permitted

137 Elm

Floors: 3

Total Occupancy: 20

Bathrooms: Shared by apartment

Coed: Yes

Residents: Mostly seniors

Room Types: Two single-studio apartments, one double-studio apartment, five double-occupancy apartments, two triple-occupancy apartments

Special Features: Private bathrooms and kitchenettes, telephone and network connection, one couch, two living room chairs, a kitchen table with four chairs, smoking permitted

148 South Professor Street

Floors: 2

Total Occupancy: 6

Bathrooms: Shared by apartment

Coed: Yes

Residents: Upperclassmen

Room Types: Six single bedrooms in one apartment

Special Features: Private bathrooms and kitchenettes, telephone and network connection, one couch, two living room chairs, a kitchen table with four chairs, smoking permitted

152 West Lorain

Floors: 2

Total Occupancy: 4

Bathrooms: Shared by apartment

Coed: Yes

Residents: Upperclassmen

Room Types: Four single bedrooms in one apartment

Special Features: Private bathrooms and kitchenettes, telephone and network connection, one couch, two living room chairs, a kitchen table with four chairs, smoking permitted

200 West College Street

Floors: 2

Total Occupancy: 4

Bathrooms: Shared by apartment

(200 West College Street, continued)

Coed: Yes

Residents: Upperclassmen

Room Types: Two single bedrooms in one apartment

Special Features: Private bathrooms and kitchenettes, telephone and network connection, one couch, two living room chairs, a kitchen table with four chairs, smoking permitted

Allencroft (Russian House)

Floors: 2

Total Occupancy: 16

Bathrooms: Shared by floor

Coed: Yes

Residents: Upperclassmen

Room Types: Singles, open doubles

Special Features: Built during the Civil War, interestingly shaped rooms, highly prized porch swing, Russian dinners, weekly Russian movies and lectures

Bailey (French House)

Floors: 2

Total Occupancy: 34

Bathrooms: Shared by floor

Coed: Yes

Residents: Upperclassmen

Room Types: Singles, divided doubles, quads

Special Features: Large lounge, small kitchen, teaching assistants from France, French films and a French petit dejeuner every other Sunday

Baldwin (Women's Collective)

Floors: 3

Total Occupancy: 35

Bathrooms: Shared by floor

Coed: No (all female)

Residents: Upperclassmen

Room Types: Singles, open doubles, two triples

Special Features: Safe space for support of feminist and women's issues, built in 1889, piano lounge, large windows, high ceilings, spacious rooms

Barnard

Floors: 2

Total Occupancy: 42

Bathrooms: Shared by floor

Coed: Yes

Residents: Upperclassmen

Room types: Singles, divided doubles, quads

Special Features: Home of Substance-Free Living, large lounge, located near center of campus

Barrows

Floors: 3

Total Occupancy: 92

Bathrooms: Shared by floor

Coed: Yes, but one section is all female

Residents: Freshmen

Room Types: Singles, open doubles

(Barrows, continued)

Special Features: Many lounges and kitchenettes, specifically designed to help students who are making the transition from high school to college

Burton

Floors: 4

Total Occupancy: 193

Bathrooms: Shared by floor

Coed: Yes, but all female fourth floor

Residents: Freshmen and upperclassmen

Room Types: Singles, open doubles, triples

Special Features: Vaulted ceilings, offices of the *Oberlin Review* and the *Grape* (both student-run campus newspapers) are located in the basement

Dascomb

Floors: 3

Total Occupancy: 156

Bathrooms: Shared by Floor

Coed: Yes, but one all-male section and one all-female section

Residents: Freshmen and upperclassmen

Room Types: Singles and open doubles

Special Features: Disability accessible, located in center of campus, dining hall, piano lounge with a Steinway grand piano, several lounges, two kitchenettes

East

Floors: 3

Total Occupancy: 187

Bathrooms: Shared by floor

Coed: Yes

Residents: Freshmen and upperclassmen

Room Types: Singles, divided doubles and quads

Special Features: Quiet hall, many singles, small lounges

East Lorain Street (20 & 22)

Floors: 3

Total Occupancy: 4 each building, (8 in total)

Bathrooms: Per apartment

Coed: Yes

Residents: Upperclassmen

Room Types: Four single bedrooms to one apartment

Special Features: Private bathrooms and kitchenettes, telephone and network connection, one couch, two living room chairs, a kitchen table with four chairs, smoking permitted

Fairchild

Floors: 3

Total Occupancy: 73

Bathrooms: Shared by floor

Coed: Yes

Residents: Freshmen and upperclassmen

Room Types: Four singles, the rest open doubles

Special Features: Lounge, co-op dining hall

Firelands

Floors: 6

Bathrooms: Per apartment

Coed: Yes

Residents: Mostly seniors

Room Types: Single studios, double, triple, quad apartments

Special Features: Converted apartment building, spacious living areas, nice kitchenettes

Harkness

Floors: 2

Total Occupancy: 64

Bathrooms: Shared by floor

Coed: Yes

Residents: Freshmen and upperclassmen

Room Types: Open doubles

Special Features: Largest co-op dining hall on campus

Harvey (Spanish House)

Floors: 2

Total Occupancy: 32

Bathrooms: Shared by floor

Coed: Yes

Residents: Upperclassmen

Room Types: Singles, open and divided doubles, quads

Special Features: Spanish movie nights, informal house study breaks and brunches, large lounge, TV lounge, kitchen

Johnson (Hebrew House)

Floors: 3

Total Occupancy: 32

Bathrooms: Shared by floor

Coed: Yes

Residents: Upperclassmen

Room Types: Singles, open doubles, two triples

Special Features: Stately mansion, spacious irregularly shaped rooms, high ceilings, large windows, Judaic library, Jewish holidays and celebrations observed

Kade (German House)

Floors: 2

Total Occupancy: 35

Bathrooms: Shared by floor

Coed: Yes

Residents: Upperclassmen

Room Types: Singles, open and divided doubles, and one quad

Special Features: Large living room, kitchen, German library, a Max-Kade German writer-in-residence

Keep

Floors: 3

Total Occupancy: 54

Bathrooms: Shared by floor

Coed: Yes

Residents: Freshmen and upperclassmen

Room Types: Singles, open doubles

Special Features: Big stone porch, lounge, fireplace, movie nights, late-night cocoa by the fire, annual Keep Halloween Party

Langston

Floors: 3

Total Occupancy: 233

Bathrooms: Shared by floor

Coed: Mostly coed, one all-female section

Residents: Freshmen and upperclassmen

Room Types: 72 singles, two super-singles, 56 divided doubles, nine quads, two super-quads

Special Features: Two quiet study lounges, two lounges for large meetings, piano, kitchenettes on each floor, TV lounge, elevator

Lord Saunders (Afrikan Heritage House)

Floors: 2

Total Occupancy: 74

Bathrooms: Shared by floor

Coed: Yes

Room Types: Singles, divided doubles, quads

Residents: Upperclassmen

Special Features: Center of activity for students who want to heighten their understanding of African, African American, and African Caribbean cultures, traditions and issues; activities typically include soul sessions, art shows, poetry nights, and the Kuumba festival

Noah

Floors: 2

Total Occupancy: 97

Bathrooms: Shared by floor

Coed: Yes

Residents: Mostly pperclassmen, some freshmen

Room Types: Singles, open doubles, triples

Special Features: High ceilings, chandeliers, lounges with fireplaces

North

Floors: 3

Total Occupancy: 233

Bathrooms: Shared by floor

Coed: Yes, but one all-female section

Residents: Freshmen and upperclassmen

Room Types: 71 single rooms for upper-class students, divided doubles, quads

Special Features: Many lounges, a second-floor "starlight room" complete with a piano and a full kitchen, a TV lounge, additional kitchenettes

North Pleasant Street (40, 62, & 66)

Floors: 2 per building

Total Occupancy: 4 each building (12 in total)

Bathrooms: Shared by apartment

Coed: Yes

Residents: Upperclassmen

(North Pleasant Street, continued)

Room Types: Four single bedrooms in one apartment

Special Features: Private bathrooms and kitchenettes, telephone and network connection, one couch, two living room chairs, a kitchen table with four chairs, smoking permitted

Old Barrows

Floors: 2

Total Occupancy: 16

Bathrooms: Shared by floor

Coed: Yes

Residents: Upperclassmen

Room Types: One single, open doubles, one triple

Special Features: Stately house with graceful columns, small co-op dining hall, near Arboretum, edge of campus

Price (Third World House)

Floors: 2

Total Occupancy: 44

Bathrooms: Shared by floor

Coed: Yes

Residents: Upperclassmen

Room Types: Singles, divided doubles, quads

Special Features: Arena for critical analysis and discussion of liberation, self-determination, and combating oppression in the West

Quadrangle (Asia House)

Floors: 2

Total Occupancy: 79

Bathrooms: Shared by floor

Coed: Yes, but one all-female section

Residents: Upperclassmen

Room Types: Singles, open and divided doubles, apartments

Special Features: Residents share interest in Asian and Asian American culture; includes lectures, films, special dinners and performances; built around open courtyard, large wood-paneled library, Pyle Inn co-op

South

Floors: 3

Total Occupancy: 234

Bathrooms: Shared by floor

Coed: Yes, but there are two all-female sections and three all-male sections

Residents: Upperclassmen

Room Types: Singles, divided doubles, quads

Special Features: Conservatory and Arts and Sciences students, lounge with piano, two kitchens, many small lounges

Talcott

Floors: 3

Total Occupancy: 78

Bathrooms: Shared by floor

Coed: Yes

Residents: Upperclassmen

(Talcott, continued)

Room Types: Singles, open doubles

Special Features: Built in late 1880s, centrally located, irregularly shaped rooms

Tank

Floors: 3

Total Occupancy: 42

Bathrooms: Shared by floor

Coed: Yes

Residents: Upperclassmen

Room Types: Singles, doubles

Special Features: Located in a more residential section of town, co-op dining hall, beautiful front yard

Union Street Housing Complex

Floors: 3 per building

Total Occupancy: 123

Bathrooms: Shared by apartment

Coed: Yes

Residents: Upperclassmen

Room Types: 30 quad apartments, and 3 quad apartments

Special Features: Furnished, most recently built

Woodland Street Houses

Floors: 10 buildings, each 2 floors

Total Occupancy: Mostly 4 in each building; 2 in 160 Woodland, 5 in 184 Woodland (39 total)

Bathrooms: One per apartment

Coed: Yes

Residents: Upperclassmen

Room Types: Four single bedrooms in one apartment; except 142 Woodland (two sets of two single bedrooms in one apartment), 160 Woodland (two singles in one apartment), and 184 Woodland (two single bedrooms in one apartment, three single bedrooms in second apartment)

Special Features: Private bathrooms and kitchenettes, telephone and network connection, one couch, two living room chairs, a kitchen table with four chairs, smoking permitted

Zechiel

Floors: 2

Total Occupancy: 40

Bathrooms: Shared by floor

Coed: Yes

Residents: Upperclassmen

Room Types: Singles, divided doubles, two quads

Special Features: Located across from Philips Physical Education Center

Room Types

Singles and Super Singles
Students share a large, central bathroom facility, but have the luxury of their own bedroom (these rooms are usually reserved for upperclassmen).

Open Doubles and Divided Doubles
Students share a large, central bathroom facility, and an open or divided bedroom (the latter offers more privacy).

Triples
Three students share a large, central bathroom facility, two bedrooms and a private living area.

Quads
Four students share a large, central bathroom facility, two bedrooms, and a private living area.

Apartments
Students share a semi-private bathroom, one bedroom, a private living area, and an in-room kitchen.

All dormitories have washing machines and dryers (students must pay to use them), communal lounges, kitchens, and bathrooms. Except for Baldwin, all dorms are coed, and have roughly the same number of women and men.

Bed Type

Twin extra-long 36"x 80," (make sure to get special sheets for these, otherwise the college will charge you an arm and a leg for their sheets).

Also Available

All-female sections, all-male sections, co-ops, program housing, quiet areas, special interest halls (for example, the Classics Hall, Science Fiction Hall), and substance-free areas

Cleaning Service?

Cleaning services—several times a week—are for public areas only, like lounges and bathrooms. For your own room, grab the vacuum cleaner down the hall (all residences have them), and keep your personal space in order.

What You Get

Bed frame and mattress, bookshelf, chairs, closet, desk, dresser, Ethernet Internet connection, free campus and local phone calls, a mirror, telephone, and window coverings

Did You Know?

A recent article in **USA Today reports that gender-neutral housing is becoming more and more common at colleges** and universities worldwide. Campuses that offer gender-neutral housing options or other gender-neutral facilities include, amongst others, Oberlin College. Revised housing policies on college campuses are part of a national movement aimed at serving the nation's transgender population.

All campus residents have access to the online Oxford English Dictionary (*www.oed.com*), JStor, and various **journal databases**.

Students Speak Out On...
Campus Housing

{ **"Talcott and Asia Quad (a program dorm), are my two favorites. You can't go too wrong, except for the really large, fairly new dorms like North Quad. The students make the dorms interesting."**

Q "**Dorms are pretty small**. Choose big dorms like South or East if you prefer quiet nights. Definitely choose Barrows for freshman year—one of the only all-freshman dorms on campus. There could be too much drama going for you there, but there's always lots of fun and beer."

Q "Dorms are varied. Talcott is a lovely 1868 house-like structure, with 12-foot-high ceilings and closets the size of dorm rooms in state colleges. **Dascomb, which houses one of the dining halls, is something of a pit**. I would highly discourage anyone from living in the all-freshmen dorms, Dascomb and Barrows. There are huge dorms—North and South—and more tight-knit, friendly dorms—Fairchild and Burton. East is a quiet dorm. That's not all of them, but it's a sampling."

Q "Dorms aren't Oberlin's strongest asset, but they vary. It's definitely possible to have a spacious and beautiful place to live your whole time at Oberlin, but **you have to know what you're doing**. Dascomb, Barrows, Langston, and South are big brick buildings that epitomize everything wrong with modern architecture. Other dorms, like Burton, Talcott, and Noah have larger and more interesting rooms, but they're harder to get. There are also a few truly awesome rooms on campus, but I'm not going to say where they are. (You have to find out on your own.)"

Q "The dorms are very dorm-like, but Talcott is old and stately (has big rooms, but poor heating), **Asia House has some great rooms** (if you can get the big ones), and J-House is beautiful, but is so far south I think it borders Kentucky. Dascomb, Barrows, and North are definitely the ones to avoid—they are obviously dorms, and too many first-years."

Q "People generally develop some serious attachment to either the north campus dorms (North or Burton), or the south campus dorms (South or program houses). Rarely do such people switch camps; I know of few such people in four years. **Try it out, get around; I advocate spending at least one night in each dorm**. And remember: Talcott probably means, 'I'm early decision,' and their parents probably attended Oberlin, as well, so watch out."

Q "Dorms are okay. East Hall is quiet and boring. Talcott is beautiful. Burton, Noah, and North are **good for meeting people freshman year**. The co-ops are also a housing option—they're not that clean, but they're cheaper, and you have more freedom (i.e. no RAs—although there are people who are there to help out with RA-type stuff), and you can pick your own roommates, and smoke in your room. It's less bureaucratic."

Q "Freshman-only or mostly-freshman dorms (Dascomb, Barrows, and sometimes the non-quiet floors of East) are great if you're a freshman, and suck if you're not. **The program houses tend to be nicer** than the regular dorms—Asia House, Baldwin, and J-House. If you're the co-op type, the housing co-ops have really nice rooms, and are less strict."

Q "**Avoid Barrows and Dascomb**. Try for Burton or Talcott."

Q "**Dascomb is a hole**. So are South, North, and Barrows. Program halls are nice, so is Barnard. Stay away from Harkness."

Q "Dascomb is a dorm that brings its residents together through deprivation. **Johnson House and Asia House** have very nice rooms in fabulous buildings, but demand at least a façade of interest in an ethnicity."

Q "**Nice dorms—Talcott, Third World, and French House**. Dorms to avoid—Dascomb, Harkness (if you're not a hippie)."

Q "Talcott is good. East is nice, too. **Barrows is fun for freshmen**—it really depends on what you make of it. I suggest East quiet floor if you have very quiet habits. I'd say avoid North because it's just so huge, and the rooms are pretty small, and it's stuck in the farthest corner on campus without having too much uniqueness to offer, (unlike the programming houses on the far end of south campus)."

Q "**Dascomb is sort of a pit from what I've heard**, but it's an excellent place to meet people if you live there. Baldwin and Talcott are beautiful, and the rooms are large with big windows. A couple of the dorms are huge and sort of anonymous, but some people like that."

Q "Nice dorms: Talcott, Fairchild, program houses, and some of the co-ops. Decent: North, South, and East. **Avoid: Dascomb and Harkness**—don't live there unless you like being dirty, and being surrounded by dirty folks— they're really nice, but they aren't super clean, if you get my drift."

The College Prowler Take On...
Campus Housing

Hands down, the ugliest dorm on campus is Dascomb Hall; however, Dascomb is conveniently located in the center of campus and is in the same building as one of the two major dining halls. As for attractive architecture, Asia House and Talcott are by far the best bet. Asia House is an old, ivy-covered, brick building, which boasts a collection of Oriental art and literature for its residents. Talcott looks more like a castle than a regular building. Firelands, a converted apartment building, is a nice alternative for upperclassmen who can't secure off-campus housing. As for students who are interested in living in a multi-lingual environment, program housing such as La Casa Hispanica, La Maison Francophone, Russia House, Hebrew House, and German House provide a great opportunity for language improvement. These living arrangements are also popular amongst students who prefer smaller-sized dormitories and a tight-knit community. In addition to the diversity of many of Oberlin's dorms, Afrikan Heritage House and Third World House provide students of color, in particular, with a safe space and a culturally-sensitive living environment.

Many students (who could otherwise not get into a single their freshman or sophomore year) find that they have a better chance of securing a single room in a program house rather than in a regular dormitory. Baldwin Cottage is a safe space for women, and the third floor of East Hall is a quiet space for students who do not enjoy raucous neighbors. Finally, Harkness, Tank, Keep, and Old Barrows are combined dormitories and food co-ops, particularly suitable for students who do not wish to eat in the on-campus dining halls.

B-

The College Prowler® Grade on
Campus Housing: B-

A high Campus Housing grade indicates that dorms are clean, well-maintained, and spacious. Other determining factors include variety of dorms, proximity to classes, and social atmosphere.

Off-Campus Housing

The Lowdown On...
Off-Campus Housing

Undergrads in Off-Campus Housing:
25%

Average Rent For:
1BR Apt.: $325 per month
2BR Apt.: $650 per month

Popular Areas:
Downtown
Lorain Street
South Professor
Woodland Avenue

Best Time to Look for a Place:
Beginning of fall semester

Students Speak Out On...
Off-Campus Housing

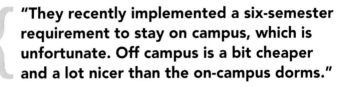

"They recently implemented a six-semester requirement to stay on campus, which is unfortunate. Off campus is a bit cheaper and a lot nicer than the on-campus dorms."

Q "You can't get off campus until you've completed six semesters. **The landlords can suck**, but for some, it's worth it for independence and party space. I will probably live on campus all four years for simplicity's sake. I won't have to worry about summer subletting, and I won't have to cook—both bonuses for me."

Q "Off-campus housing is the way to go. **It's cheaper, and you get more room**, and there are no RAs or anal-retentive hall-mates. It's only a problem if you're spoiled, and you don't want to clean your own bathroom."

Q "**Obtaining off-campus status is a notoriously obtuse process**, and you're not even allowed to try until after six semesters. But for juniors, and especially seniors, it's ideal to try and rent a house in town with some friends. Most of the good ones are well-kept, and not too far from campus. The Firelands apartment building is a nice intermediate, as long as the furniture stays all right."

Q "Pretty much all seniors can get off campus. Some juniors can. Nobody else can, unless they're married, or are violently allergic to carpets or something, which sucks, because **Oberlin's an awesome place to live off campus**. Rents are super cheap, lots of old, interesting houses and apartments, quiet streets, families who live nearby. It's infinitely better than the dorms, and really easy to work out once you're an upperclassman."

Q "If you can get off campus, do it as soon as humanly possible. **Rents are cheap**, houses are 10 times more fun, and you'll actually start feeling like you're in college and not summer camp."

Q "The college is limiting off campus more and more, so it's pretty **hard to get off-campus status**, unless you're a second semester junior or above. So by then, it's definitely worth it, because you're sick of living in the dorms, and it's way cheaper."

Q "**Can't get it until you are a junior or senior**, and unless you are willing to live way off campus, it's not worth it."

Q "**There is no off-campus housing available until junior or senior year**. The only way out of that rule is to be over 23, get married, or live with your parents in Oberlin."

Q "You can't get access to off-campus housing till after sophomore year, and even then, it's not certain. There's a lot of **variation in quality of off-campus housing**. Some is exceptional, and some is run-down stock that's not maintained by the absentee landlords. New housing for upperclass students is new for 2005–06, so there is already a significant decrease in the number of students who live off campus."

Q "I'll be living off campus next year (my senior year). Apparently, it is fairly convenient as a junior, but even with that, only so many juniors are let off campus. The college, however, owns what is known as **village-style housing**: houses and an apartment complex."

Q "All seniors have the option to live off campus, and some juniors are granted off-campus options if they're lucky. Living off campus is **more convenient and cheaper** (or about the same). I would recommend it for all seniors."

Q "Now you have to be at least a junior to get off-campus housing. I think it's **worth it for financial reasons**. Otherwise, I can see myself living in dorms throughout, unless you are a party person, and then having your own space would be desirable."

Q "ResLife has made it **hard to get off campus before senior year**. The difference between off-campus and on-campus housing really isn't that big, though. On-campus housing includes some apartments and group houses. Off-campus housing tends to be less expensive."

Q "After freshman year? No way. You'll be lucky if you get off your junior year. Seniors can get off, but do your searching early—there's enough for everyone, but **they're dumps**, for the most part."

The College Prowler Take On...
Off-Campus Housing

Once students obtain off-campus status, they are almost always glad to leave the school dormitories behind. The college recently implemented rules that make it more difficult than ever to get off-campus status, so students now have to wait until their junior, if not their senior, year before they can move out of the dormitories. Off-campus housing is a great option for those who desire a greater amount of independence and freedom, but don't forget the added responsibility that comes with living in your own home.

Living off campus gives students the opportunity to have more space and privacy, while also enabling them to hold parties that they wouldn't get away with in the dormitories. Off-campus housing varies a great deal, and it's a good idea to start looking for a place to live as early as a year before you move out of the dorms. Student houses tend to be a little run down, mostly because there is such high turn-over, and students don't always take excellent care of their abodes. On the other hand, there are many old, interesting houses with irregular-shaped rooms and cozy interiors that are of much more appeal than most of the dorms. It's also important to note that for students on financial aid, off-campus housing sometimes ends up being more expensive than on-campus housing; the college knocks $750 off of your aid package as soon as you move off campus. If you do choose to live off campus, you better get a bike, as most off-campus houses are not as close to classroom buildings as the dorms are.

B-

The College Prowler® Grade on

Off-Campus
Housing: B-

A high grade in Off-Campus Housing indicates that apartments are of high quality, close to campus, affordable, and easy to secure.

Diversity

The Lowdown On...
Diversity

Native American:
1%

White:
74%

Asian American:
8%

International:
6%

African American:
6%

Out-of-State:
91%

Hispanic:
5%

Political Activity

Most students are politically and socially liberal, some radically so. Students tend to be very outspoken about their political views, and there is hardly a day that goes by without some sort of protest, rally, or petition. Some students complain that the campus is overly politicized, while others say it is only superficial politicization, and not that radical at all.

Gay Pride

The campus is extremely accepting of its sizeable gay, transgender, transsexual, and questioning communities. One of the largest events of the year is the Drag Ball, and the school also hosts Transgender Awareness Week, and offers a fair number of Queer Studies courses. On-campus student groups, such as Queers and Allies of Faith, and LGBTU tend to be very active and outspoken. At Oberlin, it's not about tolerance, but acceptance and understanding.

Economic Status

Students come from a wide variety of socioeconomic backgrounds, though it is no secret that the majority is from predominantly middle- to upper-class families. Still, a significant number of students are on scholarships and financial aid, and those who are wealthy tend not to be showy about it.

Most Popular Religions

There are various Christian groups on campus, and a sizeable Jewish student population. There is also a Muslim Students Association, and a Pagan Awareness group, not to mention a very vocal agnostic contingent of the student population.

Minority Clubs

Minority student organizations are a strong social force on campus, and every year there are cultural shows and performances put on by various groups. The Third World House dormitory and co-op provides a safe space for students of minority or financially disadvantaged backgrounds, and the Afrikan Heritage House hosts cultural events and a political space for students of African ancestry. Every year different minority groups join together for the Colors of Rhythm dance performance.

Students Speak Out On...
Diversity

> **"Oberlin is really diverse. For a small school, people come from many different cultural and socioeconomic backgrounds, and have a plethora of different opinions and beliefs."**

Q "The campus is **pretty diverse in its own way**. I have to say, though, that it is pretty divided because of race/gender/class politics. You will probably end up eating with a lot of the same people after freshman year."

Q "Oberlin is diverse, but not evenly, which is to say, you can find just about any background and attitude here, but the majority of kids are **upper-middle-class suburbanites** who try to transcend their 'conformist' roots by wearing Carhartts and eating tempeh."

Q "It's a lot more diverse than my Midwestern high school, but not as diverse as it could be. I think the biggest problem is just that a lot of groups—social, ethnic, racial, religious, whatever—pretty much stick together, which can have benefits and consequences. But for a relatively diverse campus, a lot of my classes and housing areas are **pretty homogenous**."

Q "They tout their diversity, but I think sexual diversity isn't everything. **I'd like to see a bigger racial diversity** in general."

Q "**I wish it were more diverse**, especially income-wise, but the trend is towards richer kids getting into colleges because they can afford extra help with applications. There's a lot of multicultural stuff on campus—student organizations for every region of the world, and some administrative support. Don't miss out on shows like Dance Diaspora (African dance/drumming group), or the South Asian Students cultural show."

Q "Oberlin seems pretty diverse to me. Especially when it comes to people's beliefs and attitudes. People are generally **extremely open-minded** here."

Q "Like many small, left, liberal arts schools, the student body is **skewed towards the rich and the white**, but there is a fairly important international student body at Oberlin, as well as an African and Asian part, as well. There are also numerous sets of identical twins, which actually diminishes the diversity of the campus while rarefying it."

Q "**Fairly diverse**; it's not something I take into consideration day to day, so I have trouble commenting on it."

Q "This campus is pretty diverse, whether you're talking ethnicity, religion, or sexual orientation. In general, though, there **aren't too many people with right-wing or conservative political views**."

Q "I would say very diverse—**from the conservative to the radical**. And a considerable number of international students, myself included."

Q "**A lot of groups keep to themselves**, but between the college and the conservatory, there are a lot of very different people."

Q "Oberlin prides itself on its diversity. Most social, ethnic, religious, sexual-identity, and racial groups are represented on campus, but this is **not to imply that everyone gets along** with everyone."

Q "There are minority students at a pretty good rate considering we're a rich-kid, private, liberal arts school. But the thing is, there isn't enough mingling for my taste. **It seems like people keep to themselves** too much, which says a lot for all the activism on campus."

The College Prowler Take On...
Diversity

Diversity is an issue at the heart of most Oberlin politics. Some students say the campus is very diverse, while others complain it isn't nearly as diverse as it should be. The main point of contention comes from the fact that an overwhelming majority of Oberlin students are of European descent, and are from middle- to upper-class backgrounds. In addition, most students identify with left-leaning (and extreme left) politics, and it isn't necessarily a campus that welcomes anti-abortion or pro-Republican sentiments.

Despite a certain degree of political and class/race homogeneity, however, Oberlin does draw students from a wide variety of backgrounds. For example, you might as easily meet a football-loving flutist from Erie, Pennsylvania, or a transgendered computer whiz from New York City, as a meuroscience/religion double-major from India. The combinations of interests and talents are endless at Oberlin, and that's what makes its students so unique. The sizeable international student population, as well as the diversity of sexual orientation and identities, serves to enrich the already mixed student body.

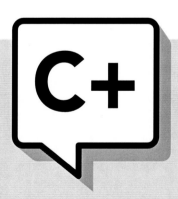

C+

The College Prowler® Grade on

Diversity: C+

A high grade in Diversity indicates that ethnic minorities and international students have a notable presence on campus and that students of different economic backgrounds, religious beliefs, and sexual preferences are well-represented.

Guys & Girls

The Lowdown On...
Guys & Girls

Men Undergrads:	Women Undergrads:
45%	55%

Birth Control Available?

Yes. Female students who have had an exam with their home doctor or have a free exam with Health Services can have their birth control prescriptions filled at Health Services for $15. Health Services also offers the Nuvaring for $15, as well as MAP for $20. In addition, Family Planning comes to Oberlin twice a week, Wednesdays and Saturdays, to offer women gynecological exams and discounted birth control. The Sexual Information Center also offers discounted safer sex supplies and free rides to clinics.

Most Prevalent STDs on Campus

HPV

Percentage of Students with an STD

Less than 10%

Social Scene

Most students at Oberlin are from the I-never-really-fit-in-in-high-school category. As a result, they tend to express their individuality as fully as possible once they get to college. Some students complain that the school is heavily segregated by cliques such as the hippies, the indie-rockers, the total geeks, and the Conservatory students (also known as "connies"). Others complain that various minority groups stick together, and that safe-spaces on campus encourage a subtle form of racial segregation. Still, most students feel they can find acceptance at Oberlin of the kind they never experienced in high school. At Oberlin, the more intellectual and off-beat you are, the cooler; the more mainstream you are, the more you can expect to feel marginalized. Still, just about everyone can find their niche at Oberlin and what is cool is often what you decide it to be.

Hookups or Relationships?

The best thing to hit Oberlin, at least insofar as relationships are concerned, is the online student dating service—although it claims to be more platonic than that—called Obiematch. Through it, students can finally figure out who that cute person in their math class is, what their major is, and where they're from. Dating at Oberlin is a tough scene with such a small student body, and a limited number of places to go on dates, but students continue to persevere—sometimes for the entire four years they are in college. Random hookups are common enough, but be warned: you'll never be able to completely avoid anyone on such a small campus. Serious relationships are fairly popular, though it's hard to get any space from your significant other when chances are, you live down the hall from each other's social circle. It's not easy to deal with a serious relationship.

Best Place to Meet Guys/Girls

Students at Oberlin are usually so involved in their studies or their music practice that they barely have time to date each other. Still, the most common way to meet someone is through extracurricular activities, study groups, or simply the people living in your dorm. Because most students place such a high priority on their academic lives, it is not uncommon for random hookups to occur. Obies often joke that the best time to meet someone is during final exam periods, when everyone is looking for some form of stress relief.

Outside of classes, the 'Sco and the Feve, not to mention off-campus parties, are great places to meet people. Winter term, especially for those students who choose to remain on campus, is also a prime occasion to up the ante on your romantic life. Some people claim that spring time is the best season to find your match, when everyone strips off a few layers and basks in the sun in Wilder Bowl, but the long and cold Ohio winters also provide ample opportunities for people to snuggle up and keep each other company.

Dress Code

Imagine a very preppy school. Now imagine its opposite, and there you have it; that's Oberlin. The best-dressed students tend to be from the Conservatory, but that's mostly because they have to spend so much time on stage, performing and auditioning. As for the college students, you can usually spot the wealthiest students by how grungy they look. Some students arrive in class wearing a bath robe, while others make a point of looking more put together. The bottom line is that, at Oberlin, anything goes. You'll find people barefoot in the rain, people dressed for a cocktail party, and people wearing every sort of mismatched clothing they can find. The only dress code is don't wear what everyone else wears.

Did You Know?

Top Three Places to Find Hotties:

1. The 'Sco
2. The Feve
3. Wilder Bowl

Top Five Places to Hook Up:

1. Off-campus parties
2. Safer Sex Night
3. The 'Sco
4. Freshman dorms
5. Drag Ball

Students Speak Out On...
Guys & Girls

"Both guys and gals are hot, in their own way. If you prefer an off-beat, hippie, relaxed, or artsy style that is not on reality TV, Oberlin will be like heaven to you."

Q "**If how hot the students are is a deciding factor** in what school you go to, you probably wouldn't have thought about Oberlin in the first place."

Q "**Guys and girls are generally pretty cool**, and sometimes hard to tell apart. But I have both female and male friends, and they all rock. All I know is, I've seen some of the most beautiful women in the world on the Oberlin campus, and if not in the 'traditional' sense, then they're beautiful in the fact that their whole selves are hotter than the sum of their parts."

Q "Oberlin attracts an interesting crew. **There's some conventional hotness**, but this is a dating community, which generally goes more for the 'beauty on the inside' than shapely, tanned legs or big muscles. Wait—did I say dating community? We're quirky about dating, but there's a fair amount of hooking up that occurs."

Q "It's a spread for both categories, and you should know that. Are they hot? I dunno, what are you into? Are you into 'indie-emo' skinny boys with too many belts? Are you into 'hippie-fabulous' kids that can smoke you stupid? Warning: there are no sorority girls or frat boys here. Well, only a few anyway, and they're probably not straight, or if they are, well, they're taken. But yeah, **there are some hotties; I spot plenty**. You notice many more during fall and spring. I think they hibernate all winter, or something."

Q "Some magazine like *Maxim* rated Oberlin one of the ugliest and least male-friendly campuses because of its feminist girls and sexual assault policy. That said, I think **Oberlin kids are hot**, and people are cool and good to be around. Lots of queer stuff, lots of straight stuff, lots of flexible stuff. There are also lots of skinny indie-rocker boys, but also normal, well-fed ones. Lots of hairy rugby girls, but also skirted dancer girls. There's a huge mix. I think we're babes; I think my friends are pretty hot. Sex goes on. People date each other. It's rough because of that one bar thing, and if you hook up with someone, you're really likely to see them immediately the next day at one of the two restaurants, but you get used to it and learn not to hate people."

Q "I'd say if you're at Oberlin, and you like Oberlin, then **Obies are probably your type**."

Q "**Guys: either you're gay or a dirty hippie**. Girls: lesbian, a dirty hippie, or a bitter straight girl who didn't realize what she was doing when she decided on Oberlin."

Q "**The average Oberlin girl is short and pudgy with dark hair**. Not all Oberlin girls are lesbians. The male-to-female ratio at Oberlin is 40:60, which leaves many desperate, yet sad, females. This is good if you are a male interested in desperate, yet sad, intercourse."

Q "**Oberlin guys are a guild unto themselves**. Stay for the weekend and find out yourself. There are no words to explain them."

Q "**This is not a dating place**, but there are definitely great people. Good to develop friendships."

Q "I think people are hot here; **people are special and confident about themselves**, in any case."

The College Prowler Take On...
Guys & Girls

Oberlin's reputation for having unattractive students is not a fair assessment. Many Obies are physically appealing, albeit in a slightly offbeat kind of way. The main styles at Oberlin fall into the following categories: crunchy hippie, indie-rock hipster, metrosexual, gender-ambiguous, and hopelessly geeky. It is occasionally possible to spot a somewhat lost-looking preppy kid, and admittedly, there are still enough jocks on campus to remind you that you are in Ohio. In short, the main lesson in style for anyone attending Oberlin is anything goes, as long as you give it a shot.

This is not to say that there aren't conventionally attractive people walking around campus, but rather that people dress in a wide variety of individual styles, and bend the norms of traditional standards of beauty. The diversity of the student population also adds a lot to the mix; girls in cowboy boots are as commonly spotted as men in shalwar kameez. Hotness at Oberlin is generally defined first by personality and physical appearance, then by originality of clothing, and finally by personal hygiene. Students in the Conservatory tend to dress better than the college students, if for no other reason than the fact that they must regularly perform in front of an audience. College students, on the other hand, are often more casual in their appearance, and on not-so-rare occasions they can be seen streaking across campus in the hottest of all styles: their birthday suits.

The College Prowler® Grade on
Guys: C

A high grade for Guys indicates that the male population on campus is attractive, smart, friendly, and engaging, and that the school has a decent ratio of guys to girls.

The College Prowler® Grade on
Girls: C+

A high grade for Girls not only implies that the women on campus are attractive, smart, friendly, and engaging, but also that there is a fair ratio of girls to guys.

Athletics

The Lowdown On...
Athletics

Athletic Division:
NCAA Division III

Conference:
NCAC

School Mascot:
Yaomen (and Yaowomen)

Men Playing Varsity Sports:
171 (13%)

Women Playing Varsity Sports:
134 (8%)

→

→

Men's Varsity Sports:
Baseball
Basketball
Cross-Country
Equestrian Sports
Fencing
Football
Golf
Lacrosse
Soccer
Swimming
Tennis
Track & Field (Indoor and Outdoor)

Women's Varsity Sports:
Basketball
Cheerleading
Cross-Country
Equestrian Sports
Fencing
Field Hockey
Golf
Lacrosse
Soccer
Softball
Swimming
Tennis
Track & Field (Indoor and Outdoor)
Volleyball

Club Sports:
Aikido
Bowling
Equestrian
Fencing
Ice Hockey
Karate-Kai
Marching Band
Rugby (Women's)
Scuba
Ultimate Frisbee (Men's and Women's)
Volleyball (Men's)
Water Polo

Intramurals:
Badminton
Basketball
Golf
Racquetball
Rugby
Squash
Table Tennis
Ultimate Frisbee
Volleyball

Athletic Fields

Dill Field, Savage Football Stadium

Getting Tickets

Tickets are free and easy to obtain; Oberlin athletes are lucky to have the spectators that they do—charging the admission would be altogether wishful thinking!

Most Popular Sports

Hands down, ultimate Frisbee draws the largest crowds. Next is women's rugby and men's soccer. IM sports are quite popular, especially when, for example, the south Asian students team is up against the Japanese students, and national rivalries spice up the game.

Best Place to Take a Walk

The Arboretum, the Kipton-Lorain Bike Trail, the Olive and Scott Carson Nature Reserve

Overlooked Teams

The men's lacrosse team doesn't get nearly the press it deserves. Also, there is a desperate need to revive the ice hockey teams—if enough students take it up again, this sport could be the most popular winter event on campus.

Gyms/Facilities

Jesse Philips Education Center
The Jesse Philips Physical Education Center is a 115,000-square-foot facility. Its gyms are used for basketball, volleyball, intramural, and other recreational activities. Other facilities in Philips include the Robert Carr Pool, climbing wall, weight rooms containing Hammer Strength, BFS, universal weight training machines, free weights, and six racquetball and eight squash courts, two of which are set up for table tennis, and one for indoor golf.

John W. Heisman Club Field House
The John W. Heisman Field House is located in the far west end of the Philips complex. It includes an indoor track with six 200-meter lanes, and four standard-sized indoor tennis courts.

Hales Auditorium
Hales Gymnasium is a separate facility from the main Philips Complex located just down Woodland Street. It contains a six-lane bowling alley, a billiards hall, and basketball court, which is home to many club and Exco classes, intramurals, and other events. It is also home to the Cat in the Cream (a student coffeehouse), a practice space, and offices for the Conservatory of Music's jazz program.

Students Speak Out On...
Athletics

> **"They are taking over now. Oberlin's new director from Stanford is transforming Oberlin from a 'jock-hater school' to an 'Ohio jock-school wannabe.' IM sports are fun and pretty prevalent."**

Q "Varsity **sports are occasionally considered a joke** on campus. We were proud to have the worst football team in the nation for several years running. I heard something like we haven't had a winning season since John Heisman coached the team. Ultimate Frisbee, on the other hand, is wildly popular. The fencing team, which is a club sport here, is active and fairly good."

Q "Nobody really cares about varsity sports on campus except for the people who are recruited to play them and their significant others. Actually, that's not entirely true, but **guest lectures have bigger attendance than football games**."

Q "**What sports**?"

Q "Sports are becoming larger on campus, or at least having a more visible presence. Games are still under attended, even though the teams are generally performing better. **IM sports are where it's at**. Spring semester softball is quite possibly the best thing in the world."

Q "**Varsity sports are somewhat big**, IM as well. I don't have much to say about it, if that gives you any idea."

Q "I think we just have a football team because the alumni association wants one. **No one really pays attention** to them."

Q "**Club sports are huge**. Varsity, no."

Q "None of the sports are big except **ultimate Frisbee**— that's either a good thing or a bad thing; I'm not sure."

Q "There are **many laughable varsity sports** on campus, but also many students inexplicably dedicated to them. Many IM sports, like soccer and basketball, have large dedicated followings and are quite popular. Badminton is a sport on the grow at Oberlin, and any student interested in badminton would do well to come to Oberlin to enrich the already vital badminton community that exists there."

Q "I really wouldn't know. **I've only been to an ultimate Frisbee game**, and that's a club sport."

Q "IM sports are fun; my softball team almost won the IM series. It was a sad day when not enough people showed, and we had to forfeit. Varsity sports are big enough that **you can probably find the sport you want to play**, but you also won't win much, most likely. Unless you join Frisbee, man, we rock at that. And football won like three games last year or something. It's got to be a record."

Q "**Sports are not big** on campus."

Q "I know for a fact we have a football team, and a soccer team, but beyond that, **IM sports are more popular**."

The College Prowler Take On...
Athletics

Most Oberlin students agree: athletics on campus are not of very much interest to anyone except to those who actively participate in them. The truth is, it's just not a jock school in any way, shape, or form. In fact, Oberlin jocks (some would go so far as to say that's an oxymoron in itself) tend to stick to themselves, much in the same way Conservatory students do. The most popular sport of all is ultimate Frisbee, and most ultimate stars tend to be sinewy and gangly-limbed, not ripped and beefy. If that isn't a sign in itself as to the status of varsity sports on campus, then what is?

No matter how apathetic Oberlin students are towards their own sports teams, athletes do have access to some excellent facilities, and can choose from a wide range of competitive sports teams. For those who aren't quite as hardcore about varsity sports, IM sports are also quite popular, and have their own followings. Because Oberlin is a liberal arts college, the focus is largely placed on education over athletics. Oberlin is not a place where athletes come to groom their talents in preparation for professional success. For that, athletes go to Ohio State. But if you are the local high school star, there are plenty of IM opportunities, as well as facilities for you to stay in shape and have some level of competition.

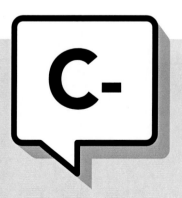

The College Prowler® Grade on

Athletics: C-

A high grade in Athletics indicates that students have school spirit, that sports programs are respected, that games are well-attended, and that intramurals are a prominent part of student life.

Nightlife

The Lowdown On...
Nightlife

Popular Nightlife Spots!

Bar Prowler:

The town of Oberlin has no clubs, and a total of only two bars. For greater variety, students sometimes make the trip to Cleveland or to any number of dive bars in Lorain County. Typically, though, Oberlin students prefer to save time and gas and go to the following bars in town:

The Dionysis Disco

Wilder Hall, West Lorain Street

www.oberlin.edu/stuorg/sco

Even though the 'Sco is open to students of any age at all times, they only serve alcohol to students over 21. Make sure to bring your student ID—they still check at the door. The 'Sco is right on campus and is really the only place around to dance. Sometimes they even host live music—but on those nights, expect a cover charge.

Feve Coffeehouse & Deli

30 South Main Street, Oberlin

(440) 774-1978

www.thefeve.com

The Feve is centrally located, and is by far the most popular drinking establishment in town. You must be 21 to get into the bar, although there is a nicely designed restaurant downstairs for those who are underage. The Feve is crowded most nights of the week, and happy hour on Fridays (between 4 p.m.–6 p.m.) is always packed with seniors.

Great Lakes Brewing Co.

2516 Market Avenue, Cleveland

(216) 771-4404

www.greatlakesbrewing.com

Though the Great Lakes Brewing Co. is pretty far from campus, it's almost worth the the trip to say you've tried their five original brews.

(Great Lakes Brewing Co., continued)

Though a bit more expensive than the local haunts, it's a great place to dine and drink because of the awesome decor—from the brewhouse tanks to the old-fashioned mahogony tap room.

The Oberlin Inn

7 North Main Street, Oberlin

(440) 775-1111

www.oberlininn.com

The Inn is most frequented by the locals, although students do sometimes drop by to get a cheap pitcher or two of beer and play a game of pool. The Inn is nowhere near as nice as the Feve, although it is often less crowded, and is at least an alternative to the one main spot in town.

What to Do if You're Not 21

On campus, the underagers can hit up the 'Sco in Wilder Hall, and the Cat in the Cream in Hales Auditorium, both on West Lorain Street. The 'Sco offers dancing, live music, and non-alcoholic beverages. The Cat in the Cream serves light beverages and snacks, and is a popular spot to hear free concerts, sketch comedy, or poetry readings. There's also the Java Zone at 5 West College Street. It's the main coffee shop in Oberlin, ever since Oberlin Music Café closed down. Many students, especially those who cannot (or do not) drink, gather there late in the evening for coffee or chai and a good conversation.

Bars Close At:

2:30 a.m.

Student Favorites:

The Feve, the Oberlin Inn, and the 'Sco. That's about all there is in the whole town. Otherwise, Cleveland is the next best bet for a stab at Ohio nightlife.

Useful Resources for Nightlife:

Cleveland newspaper, the *Plain Dealer*

Primary Areas with Nightlife:

Cleveland

Main Street in Oberlin

Cheapest Place to Get a Drink:

The Dionysis Disco

Local Specialties:

Great Lakes Brewing Co.

Other Places to Check Out:

Agave Burrito Bar and Tequilleria

Downtown Pizza

House Parties

Most students don't turn 21 until their junior or senior year, so house parties offer the best opportunity to act raucously without getting into trouble. As students get older, they tend to hold smaller, more intimate parties that run the gamut from wine and cheese gatherings to punk rock jam sessions. Some house parties charge a cover fee, anywhere from two to five dollars, the price of which usually includes free drinks.

Organization Parties

Every year, students who work for the school's radio station, WOBC 91.5 FM, host a party with live bands and plenty of indie rock to go around. Groups like Students for a Free Palestine (SFP) and the Shansi Student Organization often have campus-wide fund-raising parties, while groups like the Sexual Information Center Committee, and Ohio PIRG tend to hold more intimate, members-only parties.

Students Speak Out On...
Nightlife

{ **"Well, it's a small campus. The bar is called the Feve, and the club is on campus and it's called the 'Sco. How's that for choices?"**

 "**There isn't much in the way of on-campus parties**. Usually, the good ones are off campus. The Feve is the bar in Oberlin, and many people go there to talk and drink, but I personally like drinking in Downtown Pizza and Agave because they are less crowded, and easier to have a real conversation with a rather quiet setting."

"The nice thing about Oberlin is that you can party if you want to, and if you don't want to, you'll have no problem avoiding them. **The school runs a club called the 'Sco** (short for Dionysus Disco). There's a bar/burger place called the Feve for those over 21, and the burrito place is also a Tequilleria."

"There's really a huge variety in the parties at Oberlin. The one thing most have in common is that **there usually is great music**. Because of the Conservatory, there are lots of talented musicians around campus who are eager to play for free beer. Even if there isn't a live band, people here generally have good taste in music, so you won't ever think you're listening to top-40 radio when you're at a party."

"Parties start out great, but typically through each year, they become more clique-ish. This can be okay, though. Otherwise, learn to love **the Feve and your trusty friend, the 'Sco**. They'll always be there to comfort you at prices never to be seen outside of Oberlin."

Q "Even though there aren't any frats, every weekend there are a few student houses that buy a couple of kegs and charge admission to a few hundred kids for the chance to **get wasted, dance, and have sex**."

Q "By the time most students are juniors or seniors, they've gotten bored with the all-campus Pabst Blue Ribbon extravaganzas, and they prefer to go to smaller parties, 15 to 50 people, where everyone gets invited, and they know most of the people there. Of course, there also are a lot of students who don't party much, but instead **just hang out with a few friends**, whether it's over a board game or a pitcher of beer at the Feve."

Q "As far as bars go, **the Feve is by far the most popular**. A lot of times at Friday happy hour, it seems like everyone in Oberlin who can legally drink is there. There's also the Oberlin Inn, which is a bit lacking in ambiance, and only gets really crowded on discount pitchers night. For the kids who feel less culturally bound by their coastal suburban upbringing, there are several bars in the small towns around Oberlin that have cheap drinks, plenty of country music, and a friendly atmosphere."

Q "I don't go to a lot of parties, but the ones I've been to that haven't been too large have been pretty nice. **A lot of people have small parties**, often with themes or including a large majority of a particular student group (like OPIRG or the Frisbee team), which are pretty chill. The all-campus parties can be a little overwhelming or unyielding, but can still have some fun moments."

Q "The Feve is pretty much the only place off campus, and it's a decent bar, but being the only place causes it to be too crowded and to **charge too much for drinks**. The student union dance club, the 'Sco, offers pizza slices (from Lorenzo's), and cheap pitchers of beer on Wednesday nights. It's kind of loud and not really a place to talk to people, but it's fun to listen to bad music and play darts."

Q "I liked Oberlin parties a lot for the first three years, and then got tired of them. They tend to be at people's houses (which means crowded and stinky), and have a lot of dancing and drinking. There are usually **bands playing somewhere, which is fun and cheap**."

Q "The Feve is the only bar on campus, so there's not much of an option there unless you want to drive out to Cleveland or something. I find the college-sponsored parties (i.e. Drag Ball and Safer Sex Night) usually just get gross and crowded. The **off-campus house parties are usually pretty popular and entertaining**."

Q "There are only two popular bars in Oberlin—the Feve and the Oberlin Inn bar. The former is the student bar and is nice enough; weekends, it's packed with students. The latter caters more to the non-student population of Oberlin, and has a pool table and a Ms. Pac-Man arcade machine."

Q "I don't know of anything, really, that's off campus, except for house parties and the like, which are always really fun in their own right. There's **the on-campus bar/dance club called Dionysus Disco**, but everyone refers to it lovingly as 'the 'Sco.' Very, very cheap beer. Always fun with enough people."

Q "Sometimes the **music really rocks and the people you go with are really fun**, and then the parties are awesome. Sometimes it rains, and no one can be outside, so everyone is sweaty and crunched inside, and the band makes little sections of your brain explode, and then the parties are not as awesome."

Q "**The Feve is good**. In general, I'm not a party-goer, so I don't pay much attention."

The College Prowler Take On...
Nightlife

The town of Oberlin has a total of two bars, the Feve and Oberlin Inn. Many students lament that their debauchery must be limited to only two drinking establishments, but the lack of choice also means greater camaraderie among students. On Fridays, a large number of seniors gather in the Feve for happy hour to drink pitchers of Long Island ice tea, and eat hot tater tots and buffalo shish tavuks. The Feve was recently renovated from a somewhat dumpy bar into a more hip, swanky meeting place. Upstairs, the exposed brick walls adorned with cutting edge art gives the place a classy feel, but the thick cigarette smoke and loud music ensure a down-to-earth vibe for both students and locals.

If The Feve is full, many students choose to have a pitcher of beer or two at Oberlin Inn, where the lighting is brighter and students have a chance to mingle with Oberlin locals and play pool. During the week, students also let loose at the 'Sco, an on-campus disco that serves both alcoholic and non-alcoholic drinks. On Thursday afternoons, students enjoy unlimited free beer if they bring their professors along with them to Professor Beers. Almost as cheap is Wednesday's Pitchers Night, when beer costs only a quarter per draft! The biggest on-campus parties are the Drag Ball and Safer Sex Night. There is a multitude of other hip, on-campus parties, including Merengue Madness, and the SOCA (Students of Caribbean Ancestry) party. Both of these parties raise consciousness about Latino groups at Oberlin, while also providing students with excellent live music and a fair amount of hip shaking. All in all, Oberlin's parties are motivated by the desire to include people of all backgrounds and, most importantly, are aimed at everyone having a good time. Off-campus parties, on the other hand, tend to be somewhat more exclusive and dominated by upperclassmen.

The College Prowler® Grade on

Nightlife: C-

A high grade in Nightlife indicates that there are many bars and clubs in the area that are easily accessible and affordable. Other determining factors include the number of options for the under-21 crowd and the prevalence of house parties.

Greek Life

The Lowdown On...
Greek Life

Number of Fraternities:

0

Number of Sororities:

0

Did You Know?

Oberlin, in its more than 170-year history, **has never had a single fraternity or sorority**.

Students Speak Out On...
Greek Life

> **"No Greek life. It's awesome that way. The closest we come to the Greek system is the aforementioned co-op life. But can a co-op really be like a Greek system? Didn't think so."**

Q "It's **Greek to me**."

Q "The closest thing we have to Greek life is the Classics theme hall where they **study Ancient Greek**."

Q "People at Oberlin generally see Greek life as a way for socially insecure kids to find a sense of belonging. There's no Greek life here, and **no one misses it**."

Q "The Frisbee team is **kind of like an extremely homoerotic frat**. And Baldwin is a sorority in the sense of sisterhood, but not really like a sorority on other campuses. The only Greek life we have on campus comes from Aristotle and Aristophanes."

Q "**We don't have a Greek system**. I'm very happy about it, and I think the rest of the campus is as well."

Q "One of the best things about Oberlin is that **it has no Greek system**. Though, I think sometimes the co-ops provide their own, hippier version of frats."

Q "There is **no Greek life** to speak of."

The College Prowler Take On...
Greek Life

The students say it best! There never has been, and never will be, any Greek life at Oberlin, and just about everyone likes it that way. Oberlin is a small enough school that you don't need organized societies to meet people. There are plenty of extracurricular activities and off-campus parties, and most people at Oberlin don't like the idea of exclusive organizations in the first place.

The College Prowler® Grade on
Greek Life: N/A

A high grade in Greek Life indicates that sororities and fraternities are not only present, but also active on campus. Other determining factors include the variety of houses available and the respect the Greek community receives from the rest of the campus.

Drug Scene

The Lowdown On...
Drug Scene

Most Prevalent Drugs on Campus:

Alcohol

LSD

Marijuana

Liquor-Related Referrals:

118

Liquor-Related Arrests:

3

Drug-Related Referrals:

41

Drug-Related Arrests:

0

Drug Counseling Programs

The Counseling Center

Oberlin Health Center, Suite D
247 West Lorain Street

(440) 775-8470

Services: Counseling and psychotherapy

Office of Chaplains

Wilder Hall 217
135 West Lorain Street

(440) 775-8103

Services: Religious pastoral counseling and pastoral care

The Wellness Center

247 West Lorain Street

(440) 775-6577

Services: Individual help on a variety of topics including alternative health care, alcohol, tobacco, and other drugs

Students Speak Out On...
Drug Scene

> "I certainly have heard plenty about it, but I never experimented myself, and I never felt the slightest pressure to. Whether you do it or not it really is up to you."

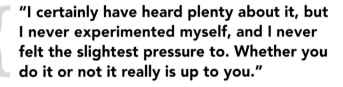 "**You can find drugs if you want to. Potheads are commonplace**, and I think north campus is more into hard drugs than south campus. I mean, some people do drugs every day, but many people just do them from time to time, or not at all."

Q "I'm personally straight-edge, and I like that drugs are definitely not pushed on this campus. If you want to find it, I'm sure you can. But **if you don't want to, it might as well not exist**. People respect your decisions here."

Q "**If you want drugs, you'll have no problem** finding them. If you don't want drugs, you'll never know they exist at Oberlin."

Q "I never drank or smoked pot before I got to Oberlin, and I certainly haven't become a drug fiend, but **I'm a lot more accepting of being around drug use** than I would have thought. The harder stuff is still kind of creepy, and I don't think it's very mainstream, though marijuana definitely is."

Q "**There are a lot of hippies**, staunch druggies, and kids with money here. Enough said."

Q "**Weed is pretty popular**."

Q "I mean, the drug scene exists. I know a few kids that have done coke, which is a real drug. **Tons of kids smoke weed or drink alcohol**, it just happens. But on the whole, kids seem to take classes seriously enough. Lots of kids smoke and, I mean, they basically all do drugs. It can be pretty lonely when you aren't really into that scene. There are kids who aren't into it either, and you end up making friends with them. It's not like the reason they don't do it is because they're socially awkward or something. At that point, it's just a personal decision."

Q "**Some drugs (pot) are pretty prevalent**, but they are not by any means the only way to socialize."

Q "I'd say **there are a lot of potheads** here."

Q "I don't think the drug scene is as big as it used to be in previous years. At the same time, yes, you'll see coke; **you'll definitely see pot**; drinking happens. Occasionally, someone on acid will run into you, literally. It's not like you necessarily have to seek drugs to get them, but at the same time, you're not confronted with them all the time."

Q "They say **it's getting harder to buy pot** around here. People smoke pot a fair amount, but not excessively. Once in a while, other drugs get in vogue. We're not close enough to a city for there to be a huge scene."

Q "I keep hearing how prevalent it is, but **I don't see all that many people wasted**."

Q "Um, that's the only thriving scene on campus. Pot, painkillers, speed, acid; **you name it, we got it**."

Q "The **biggest drug on this campus is post-modernism**. Don't do it."

The College Prowler Take On...
Drug Scene

Oberlin has no more and no less drug use than you might expect at any other affluent, liberal school of its kind. That said, most students indulge in drinking far more often than in drugs. A large majority of Obies are motivated and determined students, so drugs and alcohol are not overwhelmingly part of the social scene. Oberlin has its share of stoners, but there is very little pressure to indulge in anything besides free-spiritedness.

All sorts of drugs are available to those who want them, though pot and alcohol are by far the most prevalent. Opium may once have been a drug of choice at Oberlin, but certainly not anymore. What is certain is that many Oberlin students get hooked on caffeine, as it is the softest drug available to keep you up and working through the night. Though, there are kids on campus that prefer speed, like Adderall, coke, and meth, to keep them up. However, these more powerful stimulants often lead to other problems which Oberlin students do not have the time to deal with. There is plenty of recreational drug use, but addiction does not seem to be a problem on campus. Most importantly, even though a plethora of drugs are available to students, there is very little to no pressure to use any of these drugs. You can find potheads and straight-edge students alike at Oberlin.

C+

The College Prowler® Grade on

Drug Scene: C+

A good grade means that Drugs are not a highly-visible threat on campus. The poorer the grade, the more prominent the drug scene.

Campus Strictness

The Lowdown On...
Campus Strictness

What Are You Most Likely to Get Caught Doing on Campus?

- Drinking underage
- Public indecency
- Parking illegally
- Making too much noise in your dorm
- Streaking
- Having candles and incense in your dorm
- Downloading copyrighted materials
- Aggressively protesting

Students Speak Out On...
Campus Strictness

{ **"As long as you don't do anything too dumb, you'll be all right. Don't be publicly under the influence, and don't hurt anyone or yourself, and you should be fine. Oh, and hide your stash."**

Q "Safety and Security are there to protect you against the police. They are somehow **harder on drinking than drugs**; they think drinking is worse because people run a greater risk of getting violent."

Q "**If they see you, they catch you**; you're definitely busted."

Q "They keep saying they're going to crack down on things, but they never do. Campus **security definitely doesn't get in the way** of people having a good time, but at the same time, you can't get away with smoking a bowl in the dining hall."

Q "**Pretty lenient**: security will step in if you are possibly in a position to harm oneself or another person."

Q "It's not a dry campus. That said, **campus parties card hard**, and you won't get served without an ID. There was a drunk driving incident in the recent years that was pretty tragic, and the college has been trying to reach students about risks and stuff, but not usually in an intrusive way."

Q "If you're not loud and obnoxious, **you won't have a problem**."

Q "Safety and Security only respond if someone complains. **The town police, on the other hand, are tougher to deal with**."

Q "**They try to be strict about drinking** and stuff, but it's like trying to outlaw breathing at Oberlin."

Q "Pretty relaxed from my experience. **Campus police are much more lenient** than the town police. My friends and I once helped a student get back to her dorm room, and we were stopped by campus security. They made sure she was okay, and that we would see that she got safely to her room and check on her. So rather than slap her with drug charges, she was fine that night. The students here are responsible enough to take care of themselves, and even if they are too inebriated to do such, their friends look after them."

Q "Some of my **freshmen friends were caught drinking underage**. Not sure about drugs."

Q "I don't know anyone that went to jail or even got kicked out for that matter. **Kids rarely get busted**, but it happens."

Q "Drinking and drug **policies are enforced**, but not so strictly as to really inhibit access to alcohol or drugs."

The College Prowler Take On...
Campus Strictness

Generally, students aren't overly aware of the presence of Safety and Security officers on campus unless they explicitly ask for trouble. Many freshmen and sophomores will tell you stories about mad scrambles to hide beer when Safety and Security came knocking on their door, but that only happens if you're being too loud, or someone in your dorm knows what you're up to and decides to snitch on you. In terms of breaking up off-campus parties, Safety and Security only interferes when parties are out of hand, and neighbors complain. Obviously, if you avoid breaking policies, you won't have a problem with campus security. On the other hand, if you stay quiet and to yourself, you usually won't have any problems either.

The worst run-ins most students have with Safety and Security is if they are caught drinking underage. Oberlin has strict policies about drugs and alcohol, so if you're into any mind-and-spirit-altering substances, steer clear of on-campus events, such as Drag Ball and Safer Sex Night, when Safety and Security officers are on the lookout for mischief. Besides drugs and alcohol, Safety and Security cracks down hard on perpetrators of sexual violence—for obvious reasons. In all situations, keeping things under control is the main key to avoiding confrontations with Safety and Security. And, they are there for you if you need them or have a problem. Their main concern is the safety of the students. This may require them busting you, or busting the person giving you a hard time.

B

The College Prowler® Grade on

Campus
Strictness: B

A good grade means that Campus Strictness is not overwhelmingly present. The poorer the grade, the more strict the campus.

Parking

The Lowdown On...
Parking

Approximate Parking Permit Cost:

$60 per year

Student Parking Lot?

Yes

Freshmen Allowed to Park?

Yes

Common Parking Tickets:

Expired Meter: $5

Fire Lane: $75

Handicapped Zone: $75

No Parking Zone: $10

Parking Permits

Students using campus lots are required to register motor vehicles, and display parking permits for assigned areas. There is a $60 fee for a student to register a vehicle. All vehicles must be removed from campus at the end of the academic year.

Did You Know?

Good Luck Getting a Parking Spot Here!
The Conservatory Parking Lot

Best Places to Find a Parking Spot
Asia House Parking Lot, Athletics Field Parking Lot, Dascomb Parking Lot, and South Professor Street

Students Speak Out On...
Parking

{ **"Watch out for the snow ban, which nullifies overnight on-street parking throughout the winter. Otherwise, parking isn't too bad. After all, the campus isn't exactly a huge, bulging metropolis."**

Q "**Parking sucks**, so if you are freshman, don't bring your car. Please. I hate SUV-driving hippies."

Q "**Parking is fine until November first**. Then snow ban goes into effect. After that, you may end up walking across campus to get to your car."

Q "There's **just barely enough parking**, but it isn't always convenient."

Q "In some places, it's easy; in most others, it's not. There are few enough people with cars that I think everybody can find a spot somewhere nearby where they need to be. Mostly, **it's a walking campus**, but it's always nice to be able to get out once in a while to Cleveland or Elyria, or anywhere, for that matter."

Q "**It'd be nice to have more parking**. It's not dire."

Q "**It's not really easy**, but it's not really easy most places I've been."

Q "Pain in the butt—**there are too many cars**, especially in winter when the snow ban forbids you from street parking."

Q "**The parking scene is bumpin'**. There's usually enough parking, if you don't mind a little walk."

Q "**It's pretty awful**, actually. Especially because during the winter many of the parking lots become 'snow emergency parking,' and must be cleared of snow during the morning. Which means that you can forget about parking there overnight. I think having a car is a bit of waste of time. Then again, I have friends with cars."

Q "**There aren't that many parking places**, but not many students bring their cars, so it's easy in relation to other schools."

Q "The campus is small enough that you wouldn't want to drive to class every day! It **seems like there are enough spaces**."

Q "**It's not particularly easy to park**, but I don't think it's particularly difficult, either."

Q "**Parking is not really easy**. The parking lots are probably far away from your dorm, but you usually won't need your car anyway."

The College Prowler Take On...
Parking

Just recently, a student wrote an article to the main on-campus newspaper, *The Review*, asking that Tappan Square—Oberlin's version of Central Park—be paved over and made into a parking lot. Although his plea was obviously a joke, the fact that Oberlin has more trees than parking spaces is a source of annoyance to many vehicle-endowed students. The campus is divided into staff and student parking, and those who do not follow the rules (or the signs) finish the semester with a healthy collection of $10 parking tickets. As a result, many students decide not to drive their car to school; instead, they invest in a relatively inexpensive, multi-colored bicycle from the on-campus bike co-op, and zip around campus with their faces to the wind.

Many Obies pride themselves in being environmentally-friendly, and in order to avoid a sneer of contempt from your fellow students, it almost makes sense not to bring your car to school in the first place (especially if it's an SUV). Nonetheless, if you do own a car, count on people asking you for rides to the malls in Cleveland and Elyria, or to protests and rallies in Washington DC. Rather than pave over the lovely green grass of Tappan Square, you can split the cost of parking tickets with your friends, and still enjoy an occasional cruise through downtown Oberlin.

The College Prowler® Grade on
Parking: C

A high grade in Parking indicates that parking is both available and affordable, and that parking enforcement isn't overly severe.

Transportation

The Lowdown On...
Transportation

Ways to Get Around Town:

On Campus
Safety and Security Shuttle
Daily 9 p.m.–2 a.m.
(440) 775-RIDE

Public Transportation
Lorain County Transit (LCT)
(440) 329-5545
Pick up schedules from Wilder
Information Desk.

Taxi Cabs
Ace Taxi
(216) 361-4700
Yellow Cab Company
(216) 623-3181

Car Rentals
Alamo
local: (216) 267-4693
national: (800) 327-9633
www.alamo.com
Avis
local: (216) 265-3700
national: (800) 831-2847
www.avis.com

→

(Car Rentals, continued)

Budget
local: (216) 267-2080
national: (800) 527-0700
www.budget.com

Dollar
Local: (866) 434-2226
national: (800) 800-4000
www.dollar.com

Enterprise
local: (216) 898-2200
national: (800) 736-8222
www.enterprise.com

Hertz
local: (216) 267-8900
national: (800) 654-3131
www.hertz.com

National
local: (216) 267-4679
national: (800) 227-7368
www.nationalcar.com

Best Ways to Get Around Town

In the passenger seat of a friend's car

On a rusty bike

On a skateboard

Walking

Ways to Get Out of Town:

Airlines Serving Cleveland

Air Canada
(800) 247-2262
www.aircanada.ca

America West Airlines
(800) 235-9292
www.americawest.com

(Airlines, continued)

American Airlines
(800) 433-7300
www.americanairlines.com

Continental Airlines
(800) 525-0280
www.continental.com

Delta
(800) 221-1212
www.delta-air.com

Northwest
(800) 225-2525
www.nwa.com

Southwest
(800) 435-9792
www.southwest.com

TWA
(800) 221-2000
www.twa.com

United
(800) 241-6522
www.united.com

US Airways
(800) 428-4322
www.usairways.com

USA 3000
(877) USA-3000
www.usa3000airlines.com

Airport

Cleveland Hopkins International Airport

(216) 898-5220

The Cleveland Hopkins International Airport is 20 miles and approximately 30 minutes driving time from Oberlin College.

How to Get to the Airport

Hopkins Transportation Services Inc.

(800) 543-9912

Limousine service, prices vary.

Lorain County Transit

(440) 329-5545

Free with Student ID.
Check schedule in advance for departure times.

A cab ride to the airport costs around $45.

Greyhound

The Greyhound Bus Terminal is in Elyria, approximately 20 minutes from campus. There is also a bus terminal in Cleveland, approximately 40 minutes from Oberlin. *www.greyhound.com*

Greyhound First Express Bus Terminal

401 Lake Avenue, Elyria

(440) 322-0000

Cleveland Greyhound Bus Terminal

1465 Chester Avenue, Cleveland

(216) 781-05204

Amtrak

The nearest Amtrak station is in Elyria, approximately a 30-minute drive from Oberlin. *www.amtrak.com*

410 East River Road, Elyria

(800) 872-7245

Travel Agents

A Travel Agency

42345 Oberlin Elyria Road, Elyria

(440) 323-2600

AAA Ohio

Motorists Association
49 S. Main Street, Oberlin

(440) 774-6971

Students Speak Out On...
Transabportation

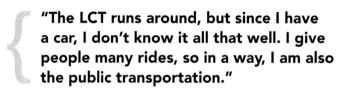

"The LCT runs around, but since I have a car, I don't know it all that well. I give people many rides, so in a way, I am also the public transportation."

Q "To get around town? **Use your feet**, or at most a bike. There isn't enough 'town' to need public transportation. To get to places like Cleveland, the LCT is available for people without cars. It's not exactly handy, but it's available."

Q "Oberlin is small enough that there's **no need to use public transportation**. The school does subsidize a public shuttle service to Cleveland commuter rail stops, and to the airport."

Q "You've **got feet**, use 'em."

Q "It doesn't really apply in such a small town. There's **Lorain Country Transit (LCT)** to get to/from the airport, and a few other places. Within Oberlin, walk or bike."

Q "The **LCT is free**, so you can get to Cleveland and the airport, and such, relatively easily."

Q "You need public transportation to get around Oberlin? Seriously, to get around Lorain County, though it is free, it's not at all convenient. If you are cool with staying in town (which you should be your freshman year), you should be fine. **You can get a bus** if you have to make a run to a mall or something."

Q "It's not convenient. **Pray you have a friend with a car**."

Q "The town is so small, **a bicycle and your feet are adequate** for day-to-day transportation. A shuttle called the LCT is available for travel into Cleveland and to the airport."

Q "**Public Transportation equals a bike**. A bike is all you need to get around town, and you can borrow one from the bike co-op."

Q "The LCT (county bus) is free. It doesn't run very often, but it isn't impossible to get out of town. To get around town, **simply walk**."

Q "Public transportation isn't very convenient, maybe once every one and a quarter hours. It's better to get a ride from someone. **Find a friend who has a car**."

Q "**Public transportation is completely unnecessary**. But the LCT is free if you want to get off campus (very convenient for getting to the airport and back)."

Q "**All you've got to do is walk**—it couldn't be more than half a mile. Or, ride your bike. We've got the LCT, but it's not that great, and not especially convenient. Make friends with someone with a car."

The College Prowler Take On...
Transportation

Students at Oberlin don't think transportation is an issue—that is, until they want to get out of town. So long as they can get what they need in Oberlin—be it shampoo, groceries, stamps, or beer—there is little need to leave town. Then again, Oberlin only has one small movie theater, two bars, and no malls, so students looking for different forms of entertainment, versus those readily available, are best off taking the Lorain County Transit into Elyria, or to the airport near Cleveland. And it is nearly a consensus that to get out of town, public transportation is not the way to go. Hopefully, you will have a friend with a car.

Besides public transportation, students also rely on their peers to give them rides into Cleveland or other surrounding towns, to go to concerts and bars, or just to get away from Oberlin for an afternoon at the Cleveland Art Museum or the Botanical Gardens. For the most part, though, students tend to be so busy with academics and social engagements at Oberlin, that the desire to get out of town is often undermined by sheer lack of time. Students who spend most of their days in Oberlin—meaning just about everyone—are happy simply using a bicycle or their own two feet to get around town. The bike co-op offers students affordable, recycled bicycles. For those who don't feel safe walking around at night, the Safety and Security shuttle is convenient and free of charge.

C

The College Prowler® Grade on
Transportation: C

A high grade for Transportation indicates that campus buses, public buses, cabs, and rental cars are readily-available and affordable. Other determining factors include proximity to an airport and the necessity of transportation.

Weather

The Lowdown On...
Weather

Average Temperature:		Average Precipitation:	
Fall:	52°F	Fall:	2.9 in.
Winter:	27°F	Winter:	2.3 in.
Spring:	47°F	Spring:	3.2 in.
Summer:	70°F	Summer:	3.7 in.

Students Speak Out On...
Weather

"All kinds of weather here; it can get pretty wet and cold in winter and very humid and hot in summer. Very windy, so a heavy, waterproof wind coat would be handy."

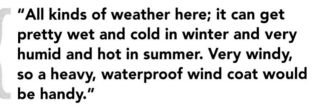 "A sweatshirt is a must because **it could drop to freezing point at any time** of the year. We don't have much of a spring or fall. We just have winter and summer."

"Early fall is lovely. The majority of the school year is **dark and cold**, with lots of snow. A good winter coat and quality snow boots are musts. Most people end up owning multiple scarves, as they are one of the few accessories anyone will actually be able to see, and are useful for identification purposes."

"The **weather changes about every three days**. I've seen six inches of snow on spring break, a freak hailstorm weeks before spring finals, 90-degree temperatures in September, anything and everything. Bring your hippiest clothes and make due. Oberlin weather is as unpredictable as it comes. Bring everything, and keep it around all year. Parka in May? Don't tempt the gods of weather here."

"There's **really beautiful weather in the fall and spring**, and a really long, cold, miserable winter with rain and snow."

"It gets very cold in the winter. Not that snowy, but **the wind chill kills**. And it's really humid in the summer. Bring a massive variety of clothes."

Q "Many blame the frequent **cloudiness and wet, cold winters** for their dislike of northern Ohio, but it's really the gloomy weather coupled with the entirely uninteresting landscape that makes northern Ohio so unenchanting. Tube tops are the preferred garment."

Q "**Winters get very cold and very, very snow-ridden**. Then it stays cold until what feels like the very last week of school. Fall is very beautiful, and so is spring. However, if you're on campus over January, the experience is unlike living out Dante's Hell. Bundle up. Invest in Ugg boots."

Q "Extremely cold winters (and pretty long). Bring warm clothes. **It can be hot during the first few months** of the school year."

Q "The weather is gray (**snowy in winter and rainy in spring**). Layers are all-important. Bring six pairs of long underwear if you're used to warmer climates."

Q "It's hot in the fall and spring, mostly pants weather. **Winter lasts a while**. Never stay on campus for winter term, or you'll want to die worse than if you lived in Moscow."

Q "The weather is the same as it is everywhere else in the Northeast and the Midwest. There are four seasons. It's cold in the winter and hot in the summer, and **gorgeous during the spring and fall**."

Q "This is the Midwest—there are four distinct seasons. Oberlin has a long, horrendous winter. Bring a big winter coat and accoutrements. It also has a nice cool fall and spring—bring lightweight stuff. And then a sweltering summer. **Bring a swimming pool**."

Q "It's pretty variable. When you first get there, it will be hot, very hot. **Come December, you'll be freezing**."

The College Prowler Take On...
Weather

Students at Oberlin never fail to be surprised by the unpredictable weather of northeastern Ohio. When students first arrive at the end of August, the weather tends to be unpleasantly balmy. Some people escape the humidity by taking a quick dip in the nearby reservoir, wearing a bathing suit or nothing at all. As the semester advances, crisp and rainy fall weather calls for a windbreaker and a sturdy pair of shoes to crunch through the leaves. Students are often surprised to see some of their peers walking barefoot along the wet sidewalks, even in chilly weather—this is just another example of Obies indulging in a spurt of free spiritedness and is nothing to be alarmed about.

The greatest test of character for students unfamiliar with a northern climate is the cold, damp winter that drapes Oberlin in a thick shroud of snow every November. For some, the winter is a blessing: it means snowball fights and romantic walks along sparkling-white fields of snow. No matter what your taste, a warm winter jacket and hat and mitts are a must. Luckily, Oberlin has a program called winter term, which means that students spend the month of January pursuing a subject of their choice anywhere in the world and are therefore able to avoid Oberlin's coldest month. Even so, for students who need a temporary distraction from the biting frost of winter or the sporadic hail of late April, a cup of hot cider from the local grocery, Gibson's, will warm anyone to the bone.

The College Prowler® Grade on
Weather: C

A high Weather grade designates that temperatures are mild and rarely reach extremes, that the campus tends to be sunny rather than rainy, and that weather is fairly consistent rather than unpredictable.

Report Card Summary

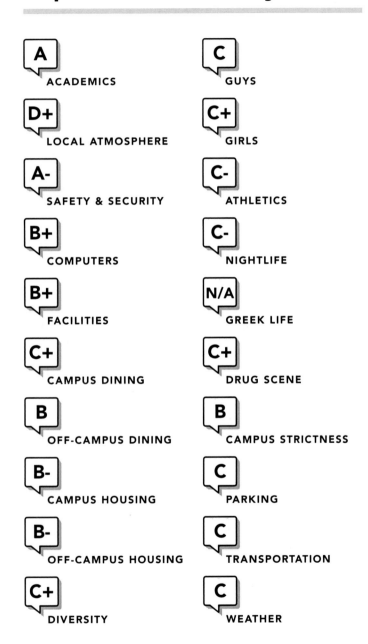

A ACADEMICS

C GUYS

D+ LOCAL ATMOSPHERE

C+ GIRLS

A- SAFETY & SECURITY

C- ATHLETICS

B+ COMPUTERS

C- NIGHTLIFE

B+ FACILITIES

N/A GREEK LIFE

C+ CAMPUS DINING

C+ DRUG SCENE

B OFF-CAMPUS DINING

B CAMPUS STRICTNESS

B- CAMPUS HOUSING

C PARKING

B- OFF-CAMPUS HOUSING

C TRANSPORTATION

C+ DIVERSITY

C WEATHER

Overall Experience

Students Speak Out On...
Overall Experience

"I would have been happy a lot of places, but there is no shortage of Excos I want to try or classes that I want to take. I thought the weather and the flat landscape would be depressing, but it's all grown on me. I like it."

"It is good. **I cannot imagine being anywhere else** besides Oberlin. If you love it, you will be in the 'bubble.' It is a sad fact that one fourth of the freshmen leave at some point without getting a diploma from Oberlin. This is not because classes are too hard, but more because they just did not fit in at Oberlin."

Q "I love Oberlin. I adore it. If I were anywhere else, I doubt I would be nearly as happy. Oberlin is definitely a finicky fit, but if it fits you, **it's a wonderful, remarkable place**. I'm getting the academic experience I always wanted."

Q "I really think Oberlin is **one of the best places to get a good college education**. Considering everything the school offers, there's no other place I'd rather be."

Q "I've liked my time at Oberlin, but I wish I could either start over, or graduate already. **It's the people I've met that are the best part**, and I've certainly had a mind-expanding experience in my classes. I am a much different person now than when I entered, but I'm still changing, so that's good. Oberlin has been a place for me to grow in every way, and it's been a long, strange, but pleasant trip so far."

Q "I've had a great experience at Oberlin, and wouldn't trade it for anything. It's odd to think that it's over; I can't imagine myself anywhere else, or with any other weird, eclectic, engaging group of people. **I've developed some serious Oberlin love and pride**."

Q "I love Oberlin. I feel challenged and stimulated by my classes and the people I meet (and also sometimes, annoyed and frustrated, though not in an inherently bad way). It's not a place to go and laze around and not leave the house—people tend to be **active and passionate about politics, art, food, sex, and everything else**. I never wished I'd gone somewhere else, and Oberlin's the kind of place that makes you want to change things if you don't like them, not just sit around. I would encourage people to go here—be open-minded and be active."

Q "**I've had my problems with it**, but I've never been unhappy enough to want to transfer. Plus, whenever I'm away for longer periods of time, I find that I miss Oberlin more than expected. So generally, yes, I'm happy with Oberlin."

Q "**I love Oberlin**. I would never want to go anywhere else."

Q "Sometimes, **I wish I could have be elsewhere**, but that comes with the territory. If you take the time to study abroad, chances are, you'll appreciate Oberlin even more."

Q "Oberlin attracts some great, interesting students along with the jerks that pepper all colleges. **Intellectual chauvinism and pomposity are the two major repellant aspects of Oberlin students**, but at least they're not bragging about how much money they make or how well they do in school. That's a good thing about Oberlin."

Q "Of the available choices, there is **nothing better than Oberlin** for me. Oberlin is good."

Q "This school is wonderful! It's not until you're outside of Oberlin that **you realize just how much the college affects you**, and the way you interact with others. You have greater tolerance for people of all backgrounds, and whether or not you are completely conscious of it, you have a greater intolerance for inequality. You find yourself volunteering and leading people, and fixing problems of any level that confront you wherever you are. I wish I were kidding, but actually, I'm rather pleased with the results."

Q "I love the people. Oberlin is definitely **a stimulating place in terms of academics**. I've met many interesting people that I wouldn't have ever known otherwise. I'm glad to be in Oberlin."

Q "I love it. **It's the best place I could have gone**. It's wonderful. Mostly, it's the people—the townies, the teachers, and the students. For the most part, they're all nice."

Q "I got more than I ever could have bargained for at Oberlin. I wanted to enrich my mind, not only academically, but also socially and spiritually. Being at **Oberlin will teach you things about yourself** that you could have never even imagined. Like I said, more than I bargained for, but I would never trade these experiences; not for the world. I feel more alive."

The College Prowler Take On...
Overall Experience

No matter how critical Oberlin students tend to be, they rarely deny the quality of education they receive. In fact, most students are more than appreciative of the unique academic and cultural opportunities Oberlin offers, and are hard pressed to think of a school they'd rather be at. Students who are frustrated with their experience often complain about the small, insular environment, long, cold winters, and the heavy workload. For those who thrive from Oberlin's stimulating academics and interesting student body, they are willing to accept the challenges inherent to attending a small, liberal arts institution. Here you won't experience the aspects of a state university education, such as Greek life, large sports, a lot of hotties, or packed classes. But that is the point. Oberlin prides itself in being everything that a state university is not.

Many students take for granted the fact that Oberlin, for an undergraduate institution of its size, has one of the most impressive library and art collections in the country, and that the Conservatory provides students with a constant repertoire of world-class music. The opportunities you will receive at Oberlin are countless, but it is up to you to find your place within the mosaic of different beliefs, interests, and passions, and to take advantage of all the available resources. Oberlin provides students with all the tools necessary for a unique and challenging experience, and can affect you to the point you realize the old Oberlin adage is true—once an Obie, always an Obie.

The Inside Scoop

The Lowdown On...
The Inside Scoop

Oberlin Slang:

Know the slang, know the school. The following is a list of things you really need to know before coming to Oberlin. The more of these words you know, the better off you'll be.

A-level – The basement floor of Mudd Library. This is where students gather for late-night study groups, last-minute essay corrections and a quick cup of coffee. It's the only part of the library where you won't get fined for having a bite to eat.

The Arb – Short for the Arboretum, a peaceful place off campus to take a walk or play Frisbee.

The Arch – The Memorial Arch in Tappan Square is a common meeting place and reference point in the middle of campus.

BBC – Abbreviation for the much-revered Brown Bag Co-op.

Commando – Intensive cleaning of a co-op in which all members must participate. The term also extends to students living off campus.

(Commando, continued)

Commando night is when all the people living in a house get together, play loud music, and scrub the whole house clean.

Conabe – Any student of the College who aspires to be in the Conservatory of Music.

Connie – Any student who is actually enrolled in the Conservatory of Music.

Co-oper – Any student who belongs to a co-op instead of the regular Campus Dining Services meal plan.

Fairkid – An abbreviation for Fairchild dormitory.

FTL – Failure to Launch; an Oberlin graduate who doesn't leave town, even after his/her degree is complete.

Harkie – Used as a synonym for hippie, this term applies to anyone who eats or lives in the Harkness Co-op and residence hall.

The Inn – The Oberlin Inn's first-floor bar; it is usually filled with more locals than students.

Mt. Oberlin – The land that was taken out when the swimming pool was excavated. It's a 30-foot high dirt mound, jokingly called a mountain because Oberlin is so flat.

Obie – Any Oberlin student or alumnus.

Obiematch – A campus-wide on-line matchmaking service.

OCMR – Oberlin College Mail Room. "What's your OCMR?" means "What's your mailbox number?"

Pitchers – Wednesday nights at the 'Sco, when beer costs only a quarter a cup!

Pomo – Any student who is a little too impressed with postmodern literary theory—quoting Jacques Derrida all the time—or someone who just dresses/acts/talks with an air of artistic pretension.

Professor Beers – When students bring their professor(s) for a drink to the 'Sco on Thursday afternoons they get free beer!

Prospie – A prospective student at Oberlin.

The Rat – Abbreviation for the Rathskellar; this restaurant/dining hall is popular amongst faculty and staff. Students need to use cash or Flex dollars to eat at the Rat.

Sexile – An unfortunate yet common occurrence at Oberlin; "sexiling" means kicking your roommate out of the room (especially open doubles) while you engage in sexual activities with one or more partners.

Special Meal – A term used in co-ops, these weekly meals usually have a creative twist to them and are a favorite, yet labor-intensive, activity enjoyed by co-opers.

Stevie – An affectionate term for Stevenson Dining Hall.

The 'Sco – An affectionate term for the Dionysus dance club and bar, located in Wilder.

The Scum – A derogatory term for the Dascomb dining hall and residence hall.

Womb Chairs – These funky, colorful, and cozy 1960s-style chairs adorn almost every floor of Mudd library.

Things I Wish I Knew Before Coming to Oberlin

- Don't buy bed sheets and linens from the school—they're expensive and low quality.

- Opt for a divided double over an open double.

- The Sexual Information Center sells safer sex supplies for really cheap.

- Bring your own bike—it comes in handy.

- If you are on work study, the best on-campus jobs are at the libraries, and working for the Student Union.

- Don't worry about going to "Disorientation" during Orientation week—it's pretty lame, and the police usually end up breaking the party up anyway.

- How exclusive certain student groups and organizations can be.

- You can take music lessons from students in the Conservatory.

- It's not a good school for people who don't like to voice their political beliefs, or hear other people's political beliefs being voiced all the time.

- First-year seminars are great! Don't overlook them.

- You can take out DVDs and VHS from the AV center on the fourth floor of Mudd for free.

Tips to Succeed at Oberlin

- Complete your distribution requirements as early as possible.
- Ask others about professors before choosing your classes.
- Don't be afraid to change advisors.
- Talk to your professors during office hours.
- Check your ObieMail e-mail account at least 10 times every day.
- Take advantage of the amazing library, the art collection, Excos, and extracurricular activities.
- Don't skip classes too often—it will catch up with you.
- Take classes in as many different departments as possible.
- Keep an open mind, but don't let critical discussion be deadened by the vice of amiability.
- If you can, study abroad one, if not two, semesters—it's a good way to see the world and refresh your opinions about Oberlin.

Oberlin Urban Legends

- A family of bats lives in the attic of Talcott and they harass students periodically.
- Someone once found a human brain in the garbage behind Asia House.
- If you step on the plaque in the middle of Tappan Square, you'll fail your next exam.
- If you pass through the Arch in Tappan Square before you graduate, you'll never graduate.

School Spirit

Oberlin students generally take pride in being conscientious thinkers. As a result, they are always finding new things about the school to complain about. Despite this fact, however, many students harbor a deep pride for Oberlin. Thus, while they may spend hours criticizing it, they will be quick to defend it in comparison with other colleges and universities. The truth is, most students recognize the quality of their college's academic and cultural life. If Oberlin apparel is any measure of school spirit, a significant number of students routinely don the letters O-B-E-R-L-I-N across their sweatshirts and T-shirts without thinking twice.

Traditions

The Big Parade
Towards the end of spring semester every year, students prepare for the Big Parade, one of the few events that successfully brings town and gown together. Students get involved by designing and painting signs, building large paper-maché puppets, and preparing martial arts/dance performances. Everyone gathers in Tappan Square to eat hot dogs or veggie burgers, watch the parade and other performances by students and townsfolk.

The Rock
Every week, new designs and messages are painted onto the six-foot-tall stone situated in Tappan Square across from the Conservatory. The tradition began in 1962, when the largest rocks in Tappan Square were painted one day before Easter. A nearby sign read: "Glacial Easter Eggs Laid by the Class of 1964." Today, both students and people in the town paint the rock with artwork, personal messages, or political statements.

A Cappella Study Breaks
Just when you think you might go nuts if you have to write one more essay or study for one more exam, Oberlin's student a cappella groups come to the rescue. Every semester, right around final exams, the Obertones, Nothing-But-Treble, and In-A-Chord gather under the ramp in front of Mudd Library to sing their hearts out and lift the spirits of their exhausted and exam-weary peers.

The Arch
Dedicated in 1903, the Memorial Arch commemorates the missionaries who lost their lives in the 1900 Boxer Rebellion in China. Today, the arch serves as the setting for Oberlin's commencement ceremonies. The arch has become a source of controversy, as some perceive it to be an emblem of cultural imperialism. In 1989, four members of the Asian American Alliance suggested that graduating seniors should walk around, rather than through, Memorial Arch during Commencement. This political statement has become a tradition for a significant number of students, and even faculty.

Clothing Swap

Every spring, students gather clothes and accessories they no longer wear or need, and donate them to the Clothing Swap program. Then, at the end of the semester, all clothes are put in Wilder Hall, where anyone may pick through them and take whatever they want. Many students find an entirely new wardrobe at the Clothing Swap, while others use it as a means of getting rid of excess layers before the summer really kicks in. It's a great way of recycling clothes!

Drag Ball

This spring event is the biggest party of the year, when the entire Student Union building is transformed into a dance hall, and people come from miles away to share in the excitement. Students often prepare for months in advance to create the most convincing drag king or queen. At the actual Ball, a celebrity drag king/queen is hired as the MC to direct the catwalk competition and judge students' elaborately designed costumes. Although the Drag Ball is a fun way of raising understanding of transgender/transsexual issues, it is also an opportunity for all students to get together under one roof.

The Art Rental Program

Each semester, the Art Rental Program allows Oberlin students to rent original works of art for a minimal fee. Many students camp out overnight in the Allen Memorial Art Museum courtyard in order to take home works by Andy Warhol, Picasso, and Toulouse-Lautrec.

Safer Sex Night

Another well-attended event is the annual Safer Sex Night, which takes place in the 'Sco, and is aimed at promoting awareness about (obviously) safer sex. This is the time when students sport their skimpiest, sexiest, and most risqué clothing and party it up with free condoms and lubricant being tossed around the room.

Finding a Job or Internship

The Lowdown On...
Finding a Job or Internship

Just about everyone at Oberlin worries about what they will do once they graduate. There are so many opportunities available, and the best place to find out about them is at the Office of Career Services. Just remember that internships over the summer and during Winter Term are an excellent way to explore your interests and passions, and make future job connections.

Advice

As early as your first semester, pay a visit to the Office of Career Services. It's never too early to start thinking about future employment opportunities, and throughout your academic career, it's a good idea to make multiple visits to the Office of Career Services. Also, be sure to attend Alumni Student Exchanges, Senior Interview Days, and the Hire Intelligence Career Fair.

Career Center Resources & Services

Alumni student exchange

Career counseling

Career services library

Career workshops

Conservatory career

Resources

e-Recruiting

Hire intelligence career fair

Oberlin online community

Placement advising

Practice interviews

Resume workshops

Senior interview days

Grads who Enter the Job Market Within

6 Months: 70%

1 Years: 77%

Firms That Most Frequently Hire Grads

ACNielsenBASES; American Institutes for Research; Bear Stearns; Credit Suisse First Boston; Federal Reserve Banks (Cleveland, Boston, etc.); Braun Consulting; Harvard Medical School; Holtzbrinck Publishing; National Institutes of Health; Teach for America; Peace Corps; Standard and Poor; The Urban Institute; Case Western Reserve University; Morgan Stanley Dean Witter; National Economic Research Associates; Skadden, Arps, Slate, Meagher & Flom; Wells Fargo

Alumni

The Lowdown On...
Alumni

Web Site:
www.oberlin.edu/alumni

Oberlin College Alumni Association:
Bosworth Hall
50 West Lorain Street
Oberlin, OH 44074
alumni.office@oberlin.edu
(440) 775-8692

Alumni Publications:
Oberlin Alumni Magazine

Services Available:
Alumni career network
E-mail forwarding
Alumni in Service to Oberlin
College (ASOC)

Major Alumni Events:
Class reunions, regional
organizations, special-interest
group reunions, and travel
tours

Did You Know?

Famous Oberlin Alumni

Jim Burrows (Class of '62) – TV director, creator of *Cheers, Frasier*

Tracy Chevalier (Class of '84) – Novelist, author of *Girl With a Pearl Earring*

Stanley Cohen (Class of '45) – Recipient of the Nobel Prize in medicine/physiology

Jerry Greenfield (Class of '73) – Co-founder of Ben and Jerry's ice cream company

Bi-khim Hsiao (Class of '93) – Legislator with the Republic of China

Larry Kleinman (Class of '75) – Organizer for Oregon's migrant workers

Caroline Kovac (Class of '74) – General manager of IBM's Life Sciences Solutions

Indira Mahajan (Class of '88) – Opera singer

Herbert Morse (Class of '65) – Chief of immuno-pathology at the National Institute of Allergy and Infectious Disease

Liz Phair (Class of '89) – Musician and singer

Jane Pratt (Class of '84) – Founder of *Sassy* and *Jane* magazines

Julie Taymor (Class of '74) – Actress and director

Laura Wendall (Class of '90) – Founder of the World Library Partnership

Student Organizations

Action (LECA)

African Students Association

Amnesty International

Anime Club

Asian American Alliance (AAA)

Astronomy Club

Chinese Student Association (CSA)

Environmental Policy Implementation Group (EPIG)

Experimental College (ExCo)

Filipino American Students Association (FASA)

Hillel

HIV Peer Counselors, Oberlin

La Alianza Latina

Lesbian, Gay, Bisexual, and Transgendered Union, OC (LGBTU)

Local Community Environmental

Middle East Students Association (MESA)

Muslim Students Association (MSA)

Nothing But Treble

Oberlin Action Against Prisons (OAAP)

Oberlin Chapter of the National Organization for the Reform of Marijuana Laws (OCNORML)

Oberlin Christian Fellowship (OCF)

Oberlin College American Civil Liberties Union (OC-ACLU)

Oberlin College Republicans

Oberlin Computer Recycling Program (OCRP)

Oberlin Film Series (OFS)

Oberlin Folk Music Club

Oberlin Gilbert and Sullivan Players (OGASP)

Oberlin Korean Students Organization (OKSA)

Oberlin Newman Catholic Community

Oberlin Peace Activists League (OPAL)

Oberlin Pro-Life Union of Students (OPLUS)

Oberlin Steel

Oberlin Stray Rescue

Oberlin Student Finance and Investment Club (OSFIC)

Oberlin Student Sierra Coalition

Oberlin Student Theater Association (OSTA)

Oberlin Swing Society (OSWING)

Obertones

OC Concert Board

OC Democrats

OC Marching Band

Offbeats

Ohio Public Interest Research Group (OPIRG)

Organ Pump Committee of Oberlin (OPCO)

Queers and Allies of Faith (QuAF)

Sexual Assault Support Team (SAST)

Sexual Information Center (SIC)

Student Senate

Students for a Free Palestine

ViBE Dance Company

WOBC-FM

The Best & Worst

The Ten **BEST** Things About Oberlin

1	Music scene
2	Clean environment
3	Art Museum
4	Library system
5	Student radio
6	Co-ops
7	Lack of sororities and fraternities
8	Liberal student body
9	Small classes
10	Winter term

The Ten **WORST** Things About Oberlin

1	Dating scene
2	Campus Dining Services (CDS)
3	No music store
4	Weather
5	Intellectual snobbery
6	Too few bars
7	ResLife
8	Unwashed students
9	Lack of anonymity
10	Flat terrain

Visiting

The Lowdown On...
Visiting

Hotel Information:

Best Western
636 West Griswold, Elyria
(440) 324-5050
www.bestwestern.com
Distance from Campus:
13 miles
Price Range: $54–$130

Comfort Inn
739 Leona Street, Elyria
(440) 324-7676
www.comfortinn.com

(Comfort Inn, continued)
Distance from Campus:
13 miles
Price Range: $60–$135

Don & Lois Harbaugh
46332 Hughes Road, Oberlin
(440) 775-1058
Distance from Campus:
1 mile
Price Range: $110–$130

➜

Econolodge

523 Griswold Road, Elyria

(440) 324-3911

www.econolodge.com

Distance from Campus:
13 miles

Price Range: $80–$110

Hallauer House B & B

14945 Hallauer Road, Oberlin

(440) 774-3400

www.hallauerhousebnb.com

Distance from Campus:
3 miles

Price Range: $100–$120

Holiday Inn

1825 Lorain Boulevard, Elyria

(440) 324-5411

www.holiday-inn.com

Distance from Campus:
13 miles

Price Range: $95–$140

Holiday Inn Express

2417 State Route 60, Vermilion

(440) 967-8770

www.holiday-inn.com

Distance from Campus:
15 miles

Price Range: $80–$100

Ivy Tree Inn and Garden

195 South Professor Street,
Oberlin

(440) 774-4510

*www.lanierbb.com/inns/OH/
17732.html*

(Ivy Tree Inn and Garden, continued)

Distance from Campus:
2 blocks

Price Range: $84–$120

Melrose Farm Bed & Breakfast

727 Vesta Road, Wakeman

(419) 929-1867

*http://homepages.accnorwalk.
com/melrose*

Distance from Campus:
13 miles

Price Range: $85–$95

Motel 6

704 North Leavitt Road,
Amherst

(440) 988-3266

www.motel6.com

Distance from Campus:
8 miles

Price Range: $39–$32

Oberlin Inn

7 North Main Street, Oberlin

(800) 376-4173

www.oberlininn.com

Distance from Campus:
Directly adjoining campus

Price Range: $60–$250

Take a Campus Virtual Tour

www.oberlin.edu/colrelat/welcome/octour/stourstart.html

To Schedule a Group Information Session or Interview

Call (800) 622-6243 on any weekday from 8:30 a.m.–5 p.m. Eastern time. Information sessions are given Monday through Saturday. Call to make an appointment for interviews or to sit in on a session.

Campus Tours

Each weekday the Admissions Office provides tours of the campus, led by current students. Tour times during the regular school year are at 10 a.m., 12 p.m., 2:30 p.m. and 4:30 p.m. on weekdays, and at 10 a.m. and 12 p.m. on Saturdays. No appointment is necessary, but the schedule does change for holidays, exam periods, and vacations, so you may wish to phone ahead.

Overnight Visits

People wanting to visit overnight have to call Oberlin's Campus Visit Office at (800) 622-6243 and ask about spending a night in the dorms as a prospective student.

Directions to Campus

Driving from the South

- Take I-71 North to the Route 250 Ashland/Wooster exit 186.
- Go west (left) on U.S. Route 250 to Ohio Route 42/250.
- Go north (right) to Ohio Route 250, turn left.
- Cross over the bridge to Ohio Route 58 north.
- Continue on Route 58 north into Oberlin.
- At the fifth traffic light, the intersection of 58 and Lorain Street (Route 511), turn left.
- At the first traffic light, turn right on to North Professor Street.
- The Admissions Office in the Carnegie Building will be on your right.

Driving from the East on I-90

- Take I-90 west to I-271 South (express or local) to I-480 West.

- Follow I-480 west to the Oberlin/Norwalk Exit for Ohio Route 10 (exit is to the left).

- Route 10 becomes Route 20. The Oberlin exit (Ohio Route 511 West) takes you into town.

- At the fifth traffic light, turn right on to North Professor Street.

- The Admissions Office in the Carnegie Building will be on your right.

Driving from the East on I-80

- Take I-80 west to exit 152 (N. Olmsted/Cleveland interchange).

- Go west on Ohio Route 10.

- Route 10 becomes Route 20. The Oberlin exit (Ohio Route 511 West) takes you into town.

- At the fifth traffic light, turn right on to North Professor Street.

- The Admissions Office in the Carnegie Building will be on your right.

Driving from the East on I-480

- Follow I-480 west to the Oberlin/Norwalk Exit for Ohio Route 10 (exit is to the left).

- Route 10 becomes Route 20. The Oberlin exit (Ohio Route 511 West) takes you into town.

- At the fifth traffic light, turn right on to North Professor Street.

- The Admissions Office in the Carnegie Building will be on your right.

Driving from the West

- Take I-80/90 to exit 135 (Vermilion Interchange).

- Turn south (right) on Baumhart Road.

- At Ohio Route 511 (flashing light) turn east (left) on Route 511 and follow it into town.

- At the second traffic light, turn left on North Professor Street.

- The Admissions Office in the Carnegie Building will be on your right.

Planning to Visit Northeast Ohio?

Still trying to figure it all out—which school, where, how do I get a complete experience? Most students need to know more. To find out about colleges in Northeast Ohio and all the region has to offer, check out *www.college360.org*.

- Visit Planning: Maps, Hotels, Driving Directions
- Information on Area Colleges
- The Internship Advantage
- Events Calendar
- Online Student Community
- What to See, What to Do, Where to Eat

Come see for yourself.

Online at *www.college360.org*

Campus Visits

There's a Web site available to help you plan your visit to colleges and universities in the Northeast Ohio region. To find out about colleges in the area and all the region has to offer, visit *www.college360.org*.

Traveling by Train?

Check out Amtrak's two-for-one discount on *www.campusvisit.com/amtrak*. Buy a ticket for a campus visit, and your parent/guardian travels free. With more than 500 destinations, you can visit almost any campus in the US.

Miles & Minutes to Local Campuses
Oberlin College to...

Baldwin-Wallace College	30 miles; 34 minutes
Case Western Reserve University	38.5 miles; 50 minutes
Cleveland Institute of Art	38.8 miles; 51 minutes
Cleveland State University	34.7 miles; 44 minutes
The College of Wooster	46 miles; 66 minutes
Cuyahoga Community College (Tri-C)	34 miles; 42 minutes
Hiram College	65 miles; 78 minutes
John Carroll University	44 miles; 55 minutes
Kent State University	62.4 miles; 74 minutes
Lake Erie College	64.1 miles; 78 minutes
Lakeland Community College	59.4 miles; 67 minutes
Lorain County Community College	14.7 miles; 24 minutes
Notre Dame College	48 miles; 58 minutes
Stark State College	77 miles; 82 minutes
University of Akron	61 miles; 68 minutes
Ursuline College	47.4 miles; 56 minutes

Words to Know

Academic Probation – A suspension imposed on a student if he or she fails to keep up with the school's minimum academic requirements. Those unable to improve their grades after receiving this warning can face dismissal.

Beer Pong/Beirut – A drinking game involving cups of beer arranged in a pyramid shape on each side of a table. The goal is to get a ping pong ball into one of the opponent's cups by throwing the ball or hitting it with a paddle. If the ball lands in a cup, the opponent is required to drink the beer.

Bid – An invitation from a fraternity or sorority to 'pledge' (join) that specific house.

Blue-Light Phone – Brightly-colored phone posts with a blue light bulb on top. These phones exist for security purposes and are located at various outside locations around most campuses. In an emergency, a student can pick up one of these phones (free of charge) to connect with campus police or a security escort.

Campus Police – Police who are specifically assigned to a given institution. Campus police are typically not regular city officers; they are employed by the university in a full-time capacity.

Club Sports – A level of sports that falls somewhere between varsity and intramural. If a student is unable to commit to a varsity team but has a lot of passion for athletics, a club sport could be a better, less intense option. Even less demanding, intramural (IM) sports often involve no traveling and considerably less time.

Cocaine – An illegal drug. Also known as "coke" or "blow," cocaine often resembles a white crystalline or powdery substance. It is highly addictive and dangerous.

Common Application – An application with which students can apply to multiple schools.

Course Registration – The period of official class selection for the upcoming quarter or semester. Prior to registration, it is best to prepare several back-up courses in case a particular class becomes full. If a course is full, students can place themselves on the waitlist, although this still does not guarantee entry.

Division Athletics – Athletic classifications range from Division I to Division III. Division IA is the most competitive, while Division III is considered to be the least competitive.

Dorm – A dorm (or dormitory) is an on-campus housing facility. Dorms can provide a range of options from suite-style rooms to more communal options that include shared bathrooms. Most first-year students live in dorms. Some upperclassmen who wish to stay on campus also choose this option.

Early Action – An application option with which a student can apply to a school and receive an early acceptance response without a binding commitment. This system is becoming less and less available.

Early Decision – An application option that students should use only if they are certain they plan to attend the school in question. If a student applies using the early decision option and is admitted, he or she is required and bound to attend that university. Admission rates are usually higher among students who apply through early decision, as the student is clearly indicating that the school is his or her first choice.

Ecstasy – An illegal drug. Also known as "E" or "X," ecstasy looks like a pill and most resembles an aspirin. Considered a party drug, ecstasy is very dangerous and can be deadly.

Ethernet – An extremely fast Internet connection available in most university-owned residence halls. To use an Ethernet connection properly, a student will need a network card and cable for his or her computer.

Fake ID – A counterfeit identification card that contains false information. Most commonly, students get fake IDs with altered birthdates so that they appear to be older than 21 (and therefore of legal drinking age). Even though it is illegal, many college students have fake IDs in hopes of purchasing alcohol or getting into bars.

Frosh – Slang for "freshman" or "freshmen."

Hazing – Initiation rituals administered by some fraternities or sororities as part of the pledging process. Many universities have outlawed hazing due to its degrading, and sometimes dangerous, nature.

Intramurals (IMs) – A popular, and usually free, sport league in which students create teams and compete against one another. These sports vary in competitiveness and can include a range of activities—everything from billiards to water polo. IM sports are a great way to meet people with similar interests.

Keg – Officially called a half-barrel, a keg contains roughly 200 12-ounce servings of beer.

LSD – An illegal drug, also known as acid, this hallucinogenic drug most commonly resembles a tab of paper.

Marijuana – An illegal drug, also known as weed or pot; along with alcohol, marijuana is one of the most commonly-found drugs on campuses across the country.

Major –The focal point of a student's college studies; a specific topic that is studied for a degree. Examples of majors include physics, English, history, computer science, economics, business, and music. Many students decide on a specific major before arriving on campus, while others are simply "undecided" until declaring a major. Those who are extremely interested in two areas can also choose to double major.

Meal Block – The equivalent of one meal. Students on a meal plan usually receive a fixed number of meals per week. Each meal, or "block," can be redeemed at the school's dining facilities in place of cash. Often, a student's weekly allotment of meal blocks will be forfeited if not used.

Minor – An additional focal point in a student's education. Often serving as a complement or addition to a student's main area of focus, a minor has fewer requirements and prerequisites to fulfill than a major. Minors are not required for graduation from most schools; however some students who want to explore many different interests choose to pursue both a major and a minor.

Mushrooms – An illegal drug. Also known as "'shrooms," this drug resembles regular mushrooms but is extremely hallucinogenic.

Off-Campus Housing – Housing from a particular landlord or rental group that is not affiliated with the university. Depending on the college, off-campus housing can range from extremely popular to non-existent. Students who choose to live off campus are typically given more freedom, but they also have to deal with possible subletting scenarios, furniture, bills, and other issues. In addition to these factors, rental prices and distance often affect a student's decision to move off campus.

Office Hours – Time that teachers set aside for students who have questions about coursework. Office hours are a good forum for students to go over any problems and to show interest in the subject material.

Pledging – The early phase of joining a fraternity or sorority, pledging takes place after a student has gone through rush and received a bid. Pledging usually lasts between one and two semesters. Once the pledging period is complete and a particular student has done everything that is required to become a member, that student is considered a brother or sister. If a fraternity or a sorority would decide to "haze" a group of students, this initiation would take place during the pledging period.

Private Institution – A school that does not use tax revenue to subsidize education costs. Private schools typically cost more than public schools and are usually smaller.

Prof – Slang for "professor."

Public Institution – A school that uses tax revenue to subsidize education costs. Public schools are often a good value for in-state residents and tend to be larger than most private colleges.

Quarter System (or Trimester System) – A type of academic calendar system. In this setup, students take classes for three academic periods. The first quarter usually starts in late September or early October and concludes right before Christmas. The second quarter usually starts around early to mid–January and finishes up around March or April. The last academic quarter, or "third quarter," usually starts in late March or early April and finishes up in late May or Mid-June. The fourth quarter is summer. The major difference between the quarter system and semester system is that students take more, less comprehensive courses under the quarter calendar.

RA (Resident Assistant) – A student leader who is assigned to a particular floor in a dormitory in order to help to the other students who live there. An RA's duties include ensuring student safety and providing assistance wherever possible.

Recitation – An extension of a specific course; a review session. Some classes, particularly large lectures, are supplemented with mandatory recitation sessions that provide a relatively personal class setting.

Rolling Admissions – A form of admissions. Most commonly found at public institutions, schools with this type of policy continue to accept students throughout the year until their class sizes are met. For example, some schools begin accepting students as early as December and will continue to do so until April or May.

Room and Board – This figure is typically the combined cost of a university-owned room and a meal plan.

Room Draw/Housing Lottery – A common way to pick on-campus room assignments for the following year. If a student decides to remain in university-owned housing, he or she is assigned a unique number that, along with seniority, is used to determine his or her housing for the next year.

Rush – The period in which students can meet the brothers and sisters of a particular chapter and find out if a given fraternity or sorority is right for them. Rushing a fraternity or a sorority is not a requirement at any school. The goal of rush is to give students who are serious about pledging a feel for what to expect.

Semester System – The most common type of academic calendar system at college campuses. This setup typically includes two semesters in a given school year. The fall semester starts around the end of August or early September and concludes before winter vacation. The spring semester usually starts in mid-January and ends in late April or May.

Student Center/Rec Center/Student Union – A common area on campus that often contains study areas, recreation facilities, and eateries. This building is often a good place to meet up with fellow students; depending on the school, the student center can have a huge role or a non-existent role in campus life.

Student ID – A university-issued photo ID that serves as a student's key to school-related functions. Some schools require students to show these cards in order to get into dorms, libraries, cafeterias, and other facilities. In addition to storing meal plan information, in some cases, a student ID can actually work as a debit card and allow students to purchase things from bookstores or local shops.

Suite – A type of dorm room. Unlike dorms that feature communal bathrooms shared by the entire floor, suites offer bathrooms shared only among the suite. Suite-style dorm rooms can house anywhere from two to ten students.

TA (Teacher's Assistant) – An undergraduate or grad student who helps in some manner with a specific course. In some cases, a TA will teach a class, assist a professor, grade assignments, or conduct office hours.

Undergraduate – A student in the process of studying for his or her bachelor's degree.

ABOUT THE AUTHOR

Writing this guide about Oberlin taught me more than I ever knew about my own school. I worked on it as I traveled in the Eastern United States and Canada, stopping to write in places like Boston, Syracuse, Montreal, North Hatley, and Pictou Island, Nova Scotia. In a few months I will be a senior at Oberlin College, completing my majors in East Asian studies (Japanese) and English, with a minor in anthropology. I grew up in Quebec, and lived in Japan for a year before starting college, so Ohio was totally new ground for me. Coming to college here has, for the most part, been an enriching and exhilarating experience. I hope the information in this guide has been useful to you in the process of making a decision about where to go to college.

Without further ado, I'd like to thank all the people who took the time to share their insight and witty commentaries about Oberlin with me: Scott, Yuuki, Bess, Logan, Rachel, Kit, Emily, Oona, Tom, Natty, Becky, David, Meaghan, Mami, and Ellen. Thank you to Dad, Mom, Pierre, Scott, Anne, Craig, Chris, and Gretchen for letting me spend so much time on your computers! Finally, thank you to the Office of Admissions at Oberlin College, the Office of Health Services, ResLife, the CIT, Safety & Security, and the Office of Career Services— where I found out about College Prowler in the first place— and to everyone at College Prowler for your help and support.

Sarah LeBaron von Baeyer
sarahlebaronvonbaeyer@collegeprowler.com

The College Prowler Big Book of Colleges

Having Trouble Narrowing Down Your Choices?

Try Going Bigger!

BIG BOOK OF COLLEGES '08
7¼" X 10", 1106 Pages Paperback
$29.95 Retail
1-4274-0001-6

Choosing the perfect school can be an overwhelming challenge. Luckily, our *Big Book of Colleges* makes that task a little less daunting. We've packed it with overviews of our full library of single-school guides— nearly 250 of the nation's top schools—giving you some much-needed perspective on your search.

College Prowler on the Web

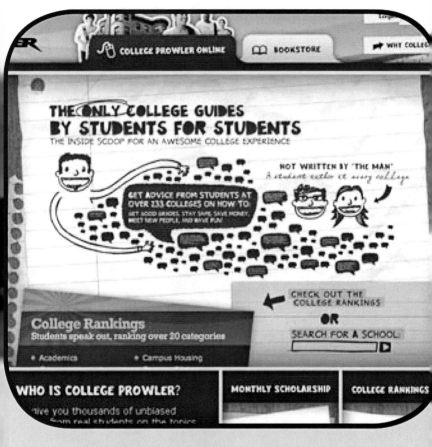

Craving some electronic interaction? Check out the new and improved **CollegeProwler.com**! We've included the COMPLETE contents of all 250 of our single-school guides on the Web—and you can gain access to all of them for just $39.95 per year!

Not only that, but non-subscribers can still view and compare our grades for each school, order books at our online bookstore, or enter our monthly scholarship contest. Don't get left in the dark when making your college decision. Let College Prowler be your guide!

Get the Hookup!

College Prowler Hookup gives you a peek behind the scenes

The Hookup is our new blog designed to hook you up with great information, funny videos, cool contests, awesome scholarship opportunities, and honest insight into who we are and what we're all about.

Check us out at *www.collegeprowlerhookup.com*

Need Help Paying For School?

Apply for our scholarship!

College Prowler awards thousands of dollars a year to students who compose the best essays. E-mail scholarship@collegeprowler.com for more information, or call 1-800-290-2682.

Apply now at **www.collegeprowler.com**

Tell Us What Life Is Really Like at Your School!

Have you ever wanted to let people know what your college is really like? Now's your chance to help millions of high school students choose the right college.

Let your voice be heard.

Check out *www.collegeprowler.com* for more info!

Need More Help?

Do you have more questions about this school? Can't find a certain statistic? College Prowler is here to help. We are the best source of college information out there. We have a network of thousands of students who can get the latest information on any school to you ASAP. E-mail us at info@collegeprowler.com with your college-related questions.

E-Mail Us Your College-Related Questions!

Check out **www.collegeprowler.com** for more details.
1-800-290-2682

Write For Us!

Get published! Voice your opinion.

Writing a College Prowler guidebook is both fun and rewarding; our open-ended format allows your own creativity free reign. Our writers have been featured in national newspapers and have seen their names in bookstores across the country. Now is your chance to break into the publishing industry with one of the country's fastest-growing publishers!

Apply now at ***www.collegeprowler.com***

Contact editor@collegeprowler.com or
call 1-800-290-2682 for more details.

Pros and Cons

Still can't figure out if this is the right school for you?
You've already read through this in-depth guide; why not
list the pros and cons? It will really help with narrowing down
your decision and determining whether or not
this school is right for you.

Pros	Cons
....	....
....	....
....	....
....	....
....	....
....	....
....	....
....	....
....	....
....	....
....	....
....	....

Pros and Cons

Still can't figure out if this is the right school for you?
You've already read through this in-depth guide; why not
list the pros and cons? It will really help with narrowing down
your decision and determining whether or not
this school is right for you.

Pros	Cons
....	....
....	....
....	....
....	....
....	....
....	....
....	....
....	....
....	....
....	....
....	....
....	....

Notes

....

....

....

....

....

....

....

....

....

....

....

....

....

Notes

....

....

....

....

....

....

....

....

....

....

....

....

....

Notes

....

....

....

....

....

....

....

....

....

....

....

....

....

Notes

....

....

....

....

....

....

....

....

....

....

....

....

....

Notes

....

....

....

....

....

....

....

....

....

....

....

....

....

Notes

....
....
....
....
....
....
....
....
....
....
....
....
....

Notes

....

....

....

....

....

....

....

....

....

....

....

....

....

Notes

....

....

....

....

....

....

....

....

....

....

....

....

....

....

Notes

....

....

....

....

....

....

....

....

....

....

....

....

....

Notes

....

....

....

....

....

....

....

....

....

....

....

....

....

Notes

....

....

....

....

....

....

....

....

....

....

....

....

....

Notes

....

....

....

....

....

....

....

....

....

....

....

....

....